A PLACE FOR TEACHER RENEWAL

**Challenging the Intellect,
Creating Educational Reform**

A PLACE FOR TEACHER RENEWAL

**Challenging the Intellect,
Creating Educational Reform**

*Anthony G. Rud Jr. and Walter P. Oldendorf,
Editors*

Foreword by Maxine Greene

TEACHERS COLLEGE PRESS

Teachers College, Columbia University
New York and London

LB
2840
.P53
1992

Published by Teachers College Press, 1234 Amsterdam Avenue
New York, NY 10027

Copyright © 1992 by Teachers College, Columbia University

All rights reserved. No part of this publication may be reproduced
or transmitted in any form or by any means, electronic or mechanical,
including photocopy, or any information storage and retrieval system,
without permission from the publisher.

Library of Congress Cataloging-in-Publication Data

A Place for teacher renewal : challenging the intellect, creating
    educational reform / Anthony G. Rud Jr. and Walter P. Oldendorf
    [editors].
        p. cm.
    Includes bibliographical references and index.
    ISBN 0-8077-3147-1 (alk. paper). — ISBN 0-8077-3146-3 (pbk. :
alk. paper)
    1. Teachers—United States—Psychology. 2. Teaching satisfaction.
3. North Carolina Center for the Advancement of Teaching.   I. Rud,
Anthony G.   II. Oldendorf, Walter P.
LB2840.P53   1992
371.1′001′9—dc20   91-28670

ISBN 0-8077-3147-1
ISBN 0-8077-3146-3 (pbk.)

Printed on acid-free paper
Manufactured in the United States of America

99 98 97 96 95 94 93 92   8 7 6 5 4 3 2 1

Contents

	Foreword by Maxine Greene	vii
	Preface	xi
1.	NCCAT's Search for a Teacher Renewal Philosophy: An Historical Account CHRISTINE M. SHEA	1
2.	Why North Carolina?: The Early History of a Teacher Renewal Effort DIANE K. HOFFBAUER	25
3.	Building a Rationale for Teacher Renewal ANTHONY G. RUD JR.	45
4.	Adventures for the Intellect WALTER P. OLDENDORF	63
5.	Administration for Human and Organizational Growth R. BRUCE McPHERSON	87
6.	The Role of Evaluation in the Development of the Center WILLIAM W. COOLEY AND WILLIAM E. BICKEL	112
7	Learning from NCCAT: An Outsider's View GARY A. GRIFFIN	128
8.	Charting the Course: The Center's Future Role in Teacher Renewal WALTER P. OLDENDORF AND ANTHONY G. RUD JR.	146
	About the Editors and Contributors	151
	Index	155

Foreword

This book is evocative of Henry David Thoreau's *Walden*, if Thoreau's text is (as it ought to be) taken as a charge to its readers to choose and renew themselves. We are challenged by that particular saunterer and explorer to "learn to reawaken and keep ourselves awake, not by mechanical aids, but by an infinite expectation of the dawn, which does not forsake us in our soundest sleep." Thoreau, after all, was concerned about persons *using* their knowledge, whether gained through books or beanfields, through roaming the woods, or through watching the snow melting and creating patterns on a wall. "The intellect is a cleaver; it discerns and rifts its way into the secret of things," he wrote. And that is it: the "secret of things"; the growth of critical insight and awareness; the perception of untapped possibility.

Yes, the chapters ahead provide detailed accounts of the distinctive Walden that is the North Carolina Center for the Advancement of Teaching. Reading the initiators, the founders, the evaluators, the participant seminar leaders, we discover a great deal about the Center's history. We find out about the "economy" of the place, the "hospitality" it offers, the ways in which dialogue is nurtured and questions passionately posed. Some of what we are told may come as a surprise: we may be startled as well as informed by accounts of teachers studying water resources, engaging in hermeneutic inquiry in mountain streams. We may wonder, perhaps in envy, at the community engagements with the arts through, for example, the design of "earthly gardens." We will be reading, we need to remember, about practicing teachers taking time out for friendship and reflection; and we will find ourselves becoming witness to their transforming themselves into eager learners, experiencing (sometimes for the first time) the wide-awakeness made possible through communication and reflective thought. Attending from the vantage points of our own situated lives, we are entirely likely to be provoked to choose dimensions of ourselves anew.

Of course there is much to learn from the writers of this book— about seminar planning, administration, evaluation, the contexts of educational reform. More important, however, is the opportunity provided for us to think about our own thinking with regard to what it means and what it ought to mean to be a teacher. Pulsating beneath the accounts of programs involving North Carolina teachers and many others is a consciousness of what it signifies for living persons actually to create identities by means of their projects, in this case projects of teaching, and—in so doing—to invent their lives. Hearing some of the voices, seeing persons constructing knowledge around their tables or on mountain roads, feeling the energies of diverse individuals in search of themselves, we cannot but realize the difference between what is conceived to be renewal and what we think of as reform.

Many of us spend our lives challenging fixity, apathy, passivity, imposition. Some of us are impatient with much of teacher education; many of us feel broken-hearted in the face of what we find in schools. And we have been reaching out for a long time to resist what demeans and petrifies. On some level we know that the teacher who is treated transitively—reformed from outside, supervised from above—is likely to become a functionary or a transmission belt. Bypassed as a person, someone with a sense of agency, such a teacher, is altogether likely to rely on the predefined, the discrete, the fixed. We realize how frequently teacher reform movements have ignored the teacher as questioner, as beginner, someone caught in wonderment and uncertainty, reaching beyond to choose and to know. Pondering the pages of this book, recalling a few bright moments of engagement at NCCAT, I think of those lines from Melville's *Moby Dick*, when the narrator talks about the impossibility of total systems, more specifically of classifying every known variety of whale. He chooses, he says, to leave his system unfinished, since grand erections, "true ones ever leave the copestone to posterity." And he concludes: "God keep me from ever completing anything. This whole book is but a draught—nay, but the draught of a draught. Oh, Time, Strength, Cash, and Patience!" Teacher renewal is equally, wonderfully incomplete; there is always, always more. Like feminist thinking too, it refuses systematization, monologism, insularity. There are more and more connections, more and more relationships to explore.

The chapters ahead open windows to diverse kinds of reciprocity, as they do to diverse possibilities of becoming for practicing teachers. In presenting teachers as learners in varied contexts, the writers here allow for multiple perspectives and multiple realities. There are, therefore, experiential adventures lying ahead for the readers of this book, adventures that treat the mind (as John Dewey said) as a verb, rather than a noun, denoting "all the ways in which we deal consciously and expressly with the situations in which we find ourselves." The Center has devised and continues to devise a great range of situations, provoking all sorts of persons to go in quest of new plans of action, new perspectives, new visions of themselves. We who read may well experience, in response, unexpected modes of mindfulness. Linking seminar rooms to mountain roads and to public spaces, scholarly effort to moral resonance, committed work to art and play, the book calls those of us in search of our own "wisdom of practice" to our own personal adventures. It makes us contemplate our own strivings to renew.

Maxine Greene

Preface

The core of *A Place for Teacher Renewal* is a study of the North Carolina Center for the Advancement of Teaching (hereafter the Center or NCCAT), an institution dedicated to teacher renewal within the broader currents of educational reform. The main themes of our argument throughout the book are that (1) the basic principles and assumptions of teacher renewal are different from the tenets of teacher or educational reform, and (2) the outcomes of renewal programs are different from those of reform programs. We will argue for ways to improve the climate for teachers' intellectual and aesthetic growth, as well as discuss specific aspects of theory and practice within our own organization.

We believe that our elementary and secondary teachers should be given the opportunity to take charge of their own growth and development. In contrast, many educational reform initiatives of the past decade imply that teachers are in some way deficient, and seek to reevaluate, to retrain, or to reeducate to remedy the deficiencies. The Center provides multiple avenues for teachers to pursue their own intellectual and creative interests, free from the structures of tests, grades, or follow-up classroom checks. We are firm in the belief that meaningful staff development begins with intellectual, artistic, and moral growth. A significant aspect of the book is our account of the successes and failures of Center programs based on these assumptions.

Throughout the book, we have tried to keep a balance between the specific and anecdotal aspects of our story and the themes that could apply elsewhere. In this way, we hope to maintain the interest and utility of this book for others who would attempt their own versions of teacher renewal. We see this volume of essays as complementary to Bolin and Falk, *Teacher Renewal: Professional Issues, Personal Choices* (Teachers College Press, 1987). Our book extends their discussion of teacher renewal by means of an institutional portrait.

Christine Shea sets the context for the book by placing the brief history and emerging philosophy of the Center in a broader framework of the history of American education and of educational thought. She draws upon work in progress to develop an alternative model for adult education.

Diane Hoffbauer follows with an account of the educational, social, and political circumstances that culminated in the establishment of the Center in 1985. Hoffbauer provides insight into the unique realities that existed in North Carolina and into the strategies that were successful in giving the Center its strong beginnings.

Anthony Rud analyzes the assumptions underlying renewal programs at the Center. He asserts that reform measures have in large part treated teachers as the purveyors of inert and approved knowledge, a stance many teachers find demoralizing. Rud relies on Dewey and others to propose the idea of the teacher as learner and inquirer as the core of a renewal program.

Walter Oldendorf examines how Center programming has evolved over 4 years in response to internal and external influences. He argues that the form and content of programs have been shaped by the original mandate of the North Carolina legislature and its interpretations by the Center staff over time, by the philosophical base articulated through discussions and writing of the Center staff, and by responses from teacher participants in Center programs. Specific examples of seminars demonstrate this threefold influence on program development, while planning now in progress points to the future shape of Center programs.

In his chapter, Bruce McPherson discusses the first five years of the administration of the Center as a new organization in which both institutional and individual priorities are equally recognized. Four explicit strategies drive the Center's internal agenda for rich human growth in the areas of learning, moral responsibility, collegiality, and commitment. McPherson details his concept of the administrator's role in promoting the active realization of an environment in which individuals can attain these goals.

William Cooley and William Bickel provide the outside evaluators' view of the Center's programs. Cooley and Bickel show how a methodology was developed to fit program design needs. They end by discussing the process of summative evaluation and the implications of that study for the impact of NCCAT.

Gary Griffin assesses the overall impact of the Center's programs by asking what can be learned from this young organization. He argues that the time was ripe for such an emphasis on teachers, while also claiming that the Center goes against the grain of educational reform in significant ways.

The editors close the book by commenting on its major themes. They discuss views of the Center's role in the state and nation and conclude with their own vision of the Center's future.

Portions of Chapter 1 were presented in different forms at the 1989 meeting of the American Educational Studies Association and the 1990 meeting of the American Educational Research Association. Portions of Chapter 3 were presented in different forms at the 1988, 1989, and 1990 meetings of the American Educational Research Association and the 1989 meeting of the American Educational Studies Association. The author would like to thank Robert Donmoyer, James W. Garrison, and Sophie Haroutunian-Gordon for their comments on earlier drafts of this chapter. The authors of Chapter 6 gratefully acknowledge the contributions of Deborah Saltrick, Pittsburgh Public Schools, for data collection and analysis for the formative research program.

We wish to acknowledge the North Carolina General Assembly and the University of North Carolina for their leadership and support of this program. We would particularly like to thank Donald J. Stedman for his guidance in the Center's formative years, and Western Carolina University for its role as host institution. Special gratitude is due to the staff of NCCAT and the teachers and administrators in the schools of North Carolina. Bruce McPherson has provided uncommon leadership for the young institution we treat in the following pages. The late Ron Galbraith of Teachers College Press encouraged this project from the beginning. Linda Lotz and Faye Zucker, and Sarah Biondello, Susan Liddicoat, and Karl Nyberg of Teachers College Press, provided expert editing and advice. Natalie Elders, Arun Jha, and Frances Stump at NCCAT added superb secretarial and research assistance. Finally, we extend our heartfelt thanks and love to Rita Rud and Sandra Oldendorf.

AGRjr	WPO
Cullowhee, NC	Dillon, MT

A PLACE FOR TEACHER RENEWAL

**Challenging the Intellect,
Creating Educational Reform**

Chapter 1

NCCAT's Search for a Teacher Renewal Philosophy: An Historical Account

CHRISTINE M. SHEA

Curriculum praxis, if it is to be guided by thoughtful reflection, must be grounded in a solid philosophical justification. This is as true for programs of teacher renewal as it is for any other area of curriculum development. If teacher renewal as an area of curriculum praxis is to develop any measure of distinctive professional identity, then practitioners need to have a clear idea about the criteria by which the success of their efforts is to be judged. Such a philosophical rationale is not merely an a priori statement of guiding principles but includes a specification of the various methods and techniques through which these criteria have been generated. The purpose of this chapter is to highlight some of the recent research completed by two NCCAT colleagues to understand the historical and intellectual underpinnings of NCCAT's teacher renewal philosophy. The emphasis in this chapter will be on curriculum development and not on organizational structure, although in previous research we have sketched out their dynamically interactive relationship (Shea & McPherson, 1990).

Teacher Renewal: A Conceptual Dilemma

Our understanding of the nature of teacher renewal contrasts with many of those available in the contemporary academic marketplace. The term "teacher renewal" has been used (and misused) in the contemporary literature to refer to teacher recertification programs. For example, an ERIC search (i.e., the computerized index of educational literature) turned up only 12 citations listed under the category "Teacher Renewal," and most of these documents entailed a description of existing recertification requirements in various state departments of education. This general usage appears to be as unfortunate as it is common and understandable. One does not have to read many documents entitled "Teacher Renewal" before concluding that these statements rarely offer much guidance to those who have experienced more complex, multifaceted dimensions in their teacher renewal programs. Historical investigations into programs of teacher renewal, too, are either fragmentary or nonexistent (Bolin & Falk, 1987; Burke, 1987; Cuban, 1984; Dickson, Saxe, et al. 1973; Ryan, 1975; Schiffer, 1980).

NCCAT stands in its infancy as a landmark experimental institution in this field. We had no exemplars to copy or wisdom of prior practice from which to learn. It was necessary, therefore, for us to pilot our own ship—to navigate the familiar educational waters but with a dramatically different mission that forced us continually to reconceptualize traditional educational pedagogies and practices. The result, we think, is unique.

Our efforts began with an attempt to look at past models of teacher education in America in order to discover whether the idea of teacher renewal as it was emerging at NCCAT had any historical precedents. Our examination of the history of teacher education highlighted something that we have become increasingly aware of at NCCAT—that there are crucial differences between programs of teacher education based on a concept of teacher reform and those based on a concept of teacher renewal. In a recent presentation, "The Teacher as Student: Lessons for Leaders," R. Bruce McPherson, NCCAT Director, cogently explicated the distinction between "reform" and "renewal."

> In my opinion, reform should focus on institutions, and renewal should be for individuals. When reform is aimed at teachers (as so much of it is today), the memory of reform *school* is conjured up, a place to change the character and personality of a miscreant. But I believe that reform is for salary schedules and governance structures, not for the souls of teachers. (1990, pp. 15-16)

He continued:

> Reform too often assumes blame, while renewal starts with faith. Reform more than occasionally targets those who seemingly are holding back progress, while alleged recalcitrance keeps the system from working effectively. Renewal assists teachers, by encouraging them and giving them strength to continue their professional efforts. To re-form is to reshape, to change fundamentally. To re-new is to restore to original quality, to count on what already exists but may be hidden. . . . Because reform focused on all of the members of the group (e.g., a school district, a school), it allows little variability in

allegiance or practices. . . . But renewal is by its nature personal, and the restoration of confidence and skill and commitment and energy varies dramatically from teacher to teacher. . . . Reform can be codified rather easily, and the dropout rate either will increase or decrease or stay the same. Renewal takes myriad forms; it is difficult to describe and assess. (pp. 16-17)

The following brief historical overview of teacher education supports and reaffirms McPherson's distinction. The focal point of interest in the early programs of teacher education was on serving the larger social order; teachers were perceived as pawns to be manipulated and controlled in order to achieve larger social goals. Teacher scapegoating is the common link in these early attempts at teacher education. Inevitably, each educational crisis was thought to be caused by teachers (the assumption being, female teachers) who were lacking some essential human attribute thought necessary to the educational endeavor—deficient traits of moral character, inadequate technical skills and behaviors, or dysfunctional emotional personality structures.

Teacher Education as Teacher Reform

In this section, I propose to review three major historical models that have been used to develop teacher education curriculum in the United States.

1. A mora. reform approach, whereby teacher education is achieved via the inculcation of certain desired traits of moral character
2. A behavioral skills reform approach, whereby teacher education is effected via the acquisition of a designated set of behavioral skills deemed congruent with effective pupil performance
3. A cultural reform approach, whereby teacher education is thought to be best achieved via the emotional adjustment of the teacher to the classroom environment

Each of these historical models also succeeded in helping us to identify and categorize one of the principal methodological orientations guiding teacher education in the school reform movement of the 1980s. In fact, one of the distinguishing characteristics of that reform movement is that all three models of teacher education received strong support by school reformers. The purpose of this review is to explain how these historical models offer inadequate and incomplete conceptualizations of the nature of teacher education. We will emphasize the ways these three pedagogical models have been more interested in *reform* than *renewal*; that is, in teacher social control and adjustment rather than any comprehensive concern with the discovery and development of human potential and individual expression in the teaching force (Shea et al., 1989).

Horace Mann's Moral Reform Movement

An examination of moral reform models of teacher education reveal that there was little interest in producing teacher educators who would engage in open public debate and dialogue over pressing social issues. Rather, the evidence shows that school reformers were concerned with limiting their school campaigns to the development of authoritarian, rule-governed character. In other words, the moral reform approach used in teacher education did not encourage teachers to confront directly questionable political practices, obvious economic injustice, or explicit criminal activities. The moral teacher was one who passively conformed to existing rules and regulations; morality was an issue of obedience to legal and religious authorities (Spring, 1986).

The major institution for educational improvement in the antebellum period was the teachers' institute, which operated as a kind of revival agency. The idea for teacher institutes was developed by Emma Willard and Henry Barnard in Connecticut during the 1830s and spread rapidly throughout the Northeast. The typical teacher institute met once or twice a year for 2 to 4 weeks. The primary objective of the institutes was to provide a brief course in the theory and practice of teaching. In his book, *The Classless Profession: American Schoolmen in the Nineteenth Century*, Paul Mattingly argues that these institutes were conducted very much like religious revivals.

> For the first generation of professional educators, this institution made explicit, more than any other educational agency, how determined schoolmen were to equate professionalization with "awakening" of moral character rather than with the training in communication skills and the standard techniques of teaching. (1975, pp. 62–63)

In fact, most of the early teacher institutes were held in the local church and were part of the same religious fervor that was known as the Second Great Awakening. Instruction in pedagogical techniques or methodologies was nonexistent or rudimentary, and the greatest emphasis was placed on elevating the moral character of the teachers. These brief teacher institutes were perhaps the earliest record in America of attention to the need for a systematic approach to teacher education. The teacher institutes spread most rapidly during the mid-nineteenth century, when the feminization of the teacher force took place.

The teacher was to be a paragon of moral virtue whose influence would be felt and imitated by the students in the common school. If the schools were to reform and morally uplift society, it was reasoned, it was of fundamental importance for teachers to function as a model of morality. Teachers were expected to live exemplary lives, with their social activities constantly under public scrutiny. The teacher institutes aimed to teach self-sacrifice, piety, discipline, and domesticity in accordance with society's view of women's destiny. Rules and regulations shaped every aspect of the women's existence; in some teacher training institutes, the school bell rang as many as 27 times a day. Morning and evening periods were spent alone in prayer and meditation; in some institutes, compulsory daily two-mile hikes, regardless of weather, were required (Melder, 1977).

This stress on the need to renew the moral character of teachers was in keeping with the general tone of other nineteenth-century reform movements. To these nineteenth-century reformers, women seemed naturally to occupy a realm of action quite distinct from that of men. In his book, *A Few Thoughts on the Powers and Duties of Women*, published in 1853, Horace Mann fell prey to the popular custom of dividing human qualities into male and female categories. As Mann wrote, "The two sexes are preordained to different spheres of action" (1853, p. 72). According to his classification, all the intuitive, domesticated, and emotional faculties were more natural to women, while all the aggressive, competitive, and intellectual characteristics were the prerogative of men.

> Any condition of society founded upon the fusion or confusion of the sexes, as though they were alike, must result in the destruction of the highest happiness of both. . . . To man God has given more strength, to women more beauty; to him more of the administrative faculty, to her more of the graces and sanctities that adorn and consecrate retirement and repose. To build up institutions for the elevation and aggrandizement of the race is his noblest ambition on earth; rightly to train up childhood is hers. (Mann, 1853, p. 72)

Like many middle class reformers of his age, Horace Mann believed that both "the idle, frivolous women" of the upper class and the lower class women subject to the drudgery of factory labor had missed their true calling. He wrote that

> They are but the diseased fruits turning into poison and unsightliness when developed in darkness.... They no more represent the true purpose and scope of women's life, than ergot represents the nutritive idea of wheat, or fungeous excrescences the rich flavor of fruit." (Mann, 1853, p. 124)

The solution, for Mann, was to return women to "the most honorable and beneficient employment in civilized society which is emphatically hers. I mean the education of children." He continued:

> That women should be the educator of children, I believe to be as much a requirement of nature as that she should be the mother of children.... The teacher's work is heart-work; yea, in the very core of the heart.... Education, then, I say emphatically is women's work; the domain of her empire, the sceptre of her power, the crown of her glory. (Mann, 1853, p. 82)

In this way, the early social reformers believed that they were only returning women to their natural sphere. Not only could they claim to be doing God's work, but they also believed that they were key figures in helping many confused female youngsters pass from an unsure adolescence into a protected feminine maturity and domesticity (Shea, 1975). This early moral reform model has continued to influence trends in teacher education programs; character education for teachers became a familiar refrain in the reform literature of the 1980s. For example, in the 1985 book *Challenge to American Schools*, Gerald Grant writes:

> The reformers of Horace Mann's generation did have a notion of a character ideal, and they drew on the examples of the founders of the Republic and on McGuffey's readers to express those ideals in ways that made a strong imprint. We cannot put McGuffey's readers back on the shelves, nor can we return to a supposed golden age. But we must have the courage to reinvent a modern equivalent of McGuffey's readers. (Bunzel, 1985, pp. 142-143)

This moral reform approach to teacher education seeks to ensure the inculcation of certain civic beliefs and behavior by stamping in or socializing certain character traits. In denying the American public school system its most crucial function as a public forum for the discussion and debates of life's most pressing moral problems and controversial issues, the heartbeat of democratic society is also silenced. In rejecting this model of teacher education, we seek to revive in our teaching force those distinctive powers of the human mind and spirit that are passionately concerned with communicating about our highest collective moral obligations and possibilities.

Technical Skills and the School Efficiency Movement

During the late nineteenth century, a second model of teacher reform emerged in conjunction with the new efficiency movement, centering around Frederick W. Taylor's program of scientific management. Taylor broke down jobs into their simplest and cheapest units and paid workers for their efficiency at completing these tasks. During the 1920s, the Taylorites' assembly line production methods became the dominant mode of factory production.

In education, the efficiency movement was based on the belief that schools and teachers could be trained to be as efficient as corporate businesses through the application of the same principles of scientific management. One of the major thrusts in these teacher education programs was the effort to reduce classroom teaching to a series of technical steps governed by something called "the new science of education." In the early part of the twentieth century, this educational movement was spearheaded by the work of Edward Thorndike and John Watson. In the 1940s and 1950s, it was elaborated by psychologist B. F. Skinner, who believed that all human behavior could be explained and controlled by planned reinforcement. Here, the individual is viewed as being controlled largely by his or her environment in the form of some stimulus–response contingency. Teacher education was viewed mainly as the process of developing specific discrete behavioral skills found to be correlated with effective classroom performance.

The first attempt to bring together systematically what was believed to be the available knowledge in the area of teacher evaluation was published in 1915 as *Methods for Measuring Teachers' Efficiency*, the 14th Yearbook of the National Society for the Study of Education (Boyce, 1915). This study is considered to be of special historical interest because it presented an overview of thinking on the topic of teacher effectiveness at the height of the school efficiency movement (Travers, 1983, p. 508). In his book, Boyce prepared a list of 150 factors judged characteristic of the effective teacher; he later reduced this to 25 factors. This early research on effective teacher behaviors, as

Robert Travers has shown, was instrumental in opening the way for other empirical studies of teacher effectiveness and led to a new interest in the design of programs for the improvement of teacher education (Travers, 1983, p. 515). During the 1920s the Commonwealth Fund provided the University of Chicago with funds to develop a new approach to teacher training under the leadership of W. W. Charters and Douglas Waples. The report of this new approach appeared in their landmark publication *The Commonwealth Teacher Training Study* (Charters & Waples, 1929). The study is remarkable in that it introduced the concept of competency-based teacher education; that is, training teachers in what were believed to be the basic competencies required for successful classroom performance.

The school reform movement of the 1980s continued this strong adherence to the principles of scientific management as embodied in the new competency-based teacher education programs for the classroom teacher. The teacher as behavioral engineer is conceived as a technician implementing a methodology devised by a team of instructional experts. Teachers are viewed essentially as passive presenters or environmental manipulators. Behaviorally oriented approaches such as these now speak about the need to have teacher education in areas as diverse as poor physical fitness, maladaptive eating habits, dysfunctional work habits, offensive language patterns, ineffective social skills, and so on. In this model, teacher education programs are usually equated with terms such as "skills refresher workshops," "technical updates," or "inservice training modules." Here, teacher education is viewed largely as the discrete learning of a series of functionally relevant work-related behaviors thought essential (even prerequisite) to effective classroom teaching. Perhaps the most urgent need for those of us interested in the evolution of more democratically based and developmentally sensitive models of teacher education is the need to reconfirm to ourselves what technical competencies can and cannot contribute to a more comprehensive theory of teacher education. Finding an appropriate role for technical skill training, and integrating it into a more comprehensive theory of teacher education, is a most essential and difficult task (Nash, 1975).

The Child-Centered Educational Reform Movement

By the turn of the century, many of the theoretical assumptions held by nineteenth-century social scientists had been either reformulated or rejected. The new liberals, for example, rejected the nineteenth-century conceptions of free will and the rationality of human action. Nineteenth-century social theorists, it was argued, had exaggerated the importance of ideas and reason; the view of man as essentially rational was perceived as hopelessly inadequate. Instead of the former belief in a fixed, rational, volitional, autonomous individual, twentieth-century American social theory increasingly argued that humans were essentially irrational and emotional beings, not at all the individuals pictured in the faculty psychology, legal system, and classical ethics of nineteenth-century America. This initial rejection of nineteenth-century concepts of rationality was followed closely by a number of attempts to develop explanations for human learning based on nonrational criteria: first, on imitation; then, on the right instinct classificatory schema of McDougall and other instinct psychologists; and later, on the conditioned reflex theories of Thorndike and Watson, culminating with the culture-personality constructs of the Chicago functionalists (Dewey, 1939; Mead, 1934; Park & Burgess, 1921).

Social decision-making theory in this realm has undergone a great transformation in the present century, and it still continues. Quite often, social interaction theories have been used to discover or create new patterns of relationships that better adjust an individual to an existing situational constraint, thereby reducing strain or anxiety. These ideas were demonstrated clearly in the new liberal constructs concerning the process of cultural socialization. Those theories stressed that each cultural group developed a unique process for inducting its young into group life. This process of cultural socialization was believed to be particularly important in shaping attitudes, emotions, and temperaments. The cultural environment of the home provided the earliest and, according to new liberal social scientists, the most thorough and lasting socialization for the child's personality (Iowa Child Welfare Research Station, University of Iowa, 1933, 1967). In particular, it was claimed, the emotional climate of the home and the school was shaped largely by the quality of the parent–child/teacher–child relationship. On the basis of these consistently repeated interactions, children in time built up those emotional attitudes and predispositions that constituted their personalities. These understandings led to questions about the kinds of character and personality temperaments that could be fostered by certain methods of child rearing and teacher education (Blatz, 1944; Cooley, 1909; Mead, 1934; Sherman, 1938).

Considerable confusion was injected by the Federal Office of Education, which became enamored with the idea of "emotional adjustment" during the 1920s and 1930s. Just how the federal government became involved in the sponsorship of such a vague idea is not clear, but it did produce bulletin after bulletin that promoted the concept of emotional adjustment as the key to effective education. Emotional disorders in children were essentially symptoms of their particular cultural environments. What this viewpoint implied, therefore, was that an abusive childhood tended to create a personality characterized by anxiety, guilt, hostility, or aggressiveness. These dysfunctional emotional complexes could subsequently be reflected in any number of socially acceptable or unacceptable conditions; that is, in physical illness, mental disorders, or various forms of crime, delinquency, sexual offenses, and the like (White House Conference on Child Health and Protection, 1936).

The school reform movement of the 1980s utilized a similar mental health model. Staff development and teacher burnout literature tends to locate the problem of teacher education where its symptoms are most evident, that is, in the emotional problems of individual teachers. Remedies are designed, therefore, to train stress-prone professionals to cope with the pressures of school life, not to make teachers' work less stressful. In their recent research, Webb and Ashton cite one expert, Al Cedoline, who, while acknowledging that negative work settings contribute to job stress, described burned out professionals as cynical, inflexible, resistant to change, subtly paranoid, emotionally fatigued, irritable, accident-prone individuals who had not learned to cope adequately with the realities of everyday life (Webb & Ashton, 1979, p. 32). He suggested that administrators help teachers learn to cope with stress by offering programs in meditation, progressive relaxation, thought-intrusion exercises, focused breathing, desensitization, yoga, biofeedback, and more. He also advised teachers to learn to control their griping, to be more effective disciplinarians, to improve their communication skills, to develop emotive attitudes of "detached concern" for students, and to look pleasant in their encounters with students, teachers, and administrators.

At a time when so many educators suffer from the stressful effects of their teaching environments, it is difficult to critique programs that may bring some relief, no matter how superficial they may be. Yet, NCCAT's own research with teachers suggests that their dissatisfactions are often caused not by their own maladaptive responses to their work, but rather by the circumstances in which they are expected to perform their duties (Cooley, 1989). The sheer number of teachers who report that they are unhappy with their work, as Webb and Ashton also suggest, implies that teacher burnout is a structural rather than a personal dysfunction (Webb & Ashton, 1979, p. 33). This finding is especially instructive.

Teacher Education: A Retrospective Critique

This brief survey highlights some major difficulties with historical models of teacher education.

First, I observed that one of the most frequently committed errors by adherents to these various teacher education models is that of *disciplinary imperialism*—the tendency to assert inflated claims for the problem-solving capacity of one's own area of expertise and the tendency to ignore (or trivialize) problems that are not amenable to solution within one's particular disciplinary realm.

Second, each of the perspectives in my historical research succeeded in helping to classify and categorize one of the major teacher renewal components—which is why, ultimately, each perspective must be recognized as an important part of a more comprehensive theory of teacher education. Thus, we interpret the concept of teacher education broadly, arguing that its meanings are of many kinds and that a full and complete human development program requires education in a variety of realms rather than a single type of competence. Teacher education is more than the acquisition of technical proficiency, more than moral awakening, more than building self-esteem and emotional stability.

Third, the history of teacher education highlights the extent to which the emphasis in teacher reform programs has always been on changing some deviant trait of moral character, inadequate technical skill, or supposedly dysfunctional emotional personality structure. The focal point of interest in these programs has always been on the larger social order; teachers were often perceived as pawns to be manipulated and socially controlled in order to achieve greater social goals. Thus, from this perspective, we must be aware in developing a more comprehensive theory of teacher education that we not mistake a symptom for a cause, and thereby subtly shift the blame for these various dysfunctions from oppressive school structures and environments to the victims.

Fourth, there is a failure to define adequately what constitutes a good teacher. An implicit assumption in my research is that a good teacher really does employ different ways of knowing in operating a successful and valuable classroom program. Therefore, any comprehensive theory of teacher education must renew and restore teachers to these various levels of teaching effectiveness and expertise. This position also assumes that there is a direct connection between the process of developing a good teacher and the process of educating a person to a full and complete development of his or her human capabilities—emotional, social, intellectual, moral, and aesthetic.

Teacher Education as Teacher Renewal

These historical investigations point to the need for a more comprehensive concept of teacher education. Thus, while teacher education should focus on individuals, should this education focus on the individual as largely a moral, cognitive, or emotive being? I shall argue on the basis of the Shea-McPherson model of adult education (Shea & McPherson, 1990) for a more comprehensive concept of teacher education. Our investigations led us to a number of conclusions. First, there is a need for a new paradigm of teacher education that will integrate rather than replace existent teacher education paradigms and overcome some of the problems that exist within, and especially between, these various models. Second, these studies also led us to assert that there is a fourth realm, the aesthetic mode, that has not been adequately described or conceptualized as an essential element in the teacher education literature. Third, we concluded that our emerging NCCAT philosophy of teacher renewal, not the historical precedent of teacher reform, should form the basis for any comprehensive program of teacher education (McPherson, 1990; McPherson, Crowson, & Pitner, 1986; Shea & McPherson, 1990, forthcoming).

Criteria for a Good Teacher Renewal Philosophy

Our efforts then turned to an attempt to articulate what we understood to be the criteria for a good philosophical theory. If the purpose of philosophy is to provide a rationally justified world view, we reasoned, then a good teacher education philosophy must likewise satisfy a number of basic criteria. In our previous research, we elaborated, on the basis of lengthy ethnographic documentation of the NCCAT seminar process and via a detailed reconceptualization and extension of Habermas's work (1971, 1973), four basic cognitive processes that we concluded form the underlying framework of NCCAT's model of adult education. A good teacher renewal philosophy, we concluded, must provide

1. A process for articulating a reliable understanding of the nature of reality (i.e., the realm of the empirical sciences and analytic philosophy)
2. A process for articulating the human significance of this reality (i.e., the realm of cultural sociology)
3. An ethical schema for generating common social ideals (i.e., the realm of ethics and politics)

4. A personal dialogical praxis for overcoming or minimizing the identified discrepancies between the common social ideals and the actual state of affairs (i.e., the realm of personal aesthetic praxis)

Our own approach demands one addendum—a good teacher renewal philosophy, we thought, should take into account the feelings, desires, aspirations, and motives of an individual at a particular historical juncture, both present capacities and limitations. Therefore, a good teacher renewal philosophy should help a teacher resolve his or her day-to-day problems through practical solutions that are both emotionally satisfying and aesthetically pleasing to the individual. In sum, we think a good teacher renewal philosophy ought to be rational, true, morally justifiable, emotionally satisfying, and aesthetically pleasing. We called this unified collective framework our "meaning-making structure," and the product of such deliberations "creative wisdom" (Shea & McPherson, 1990).

In this section, the basic underlying components of the various realms of meaning will be summarized, showing how each embodies a certain kind of conceptual discrimination, component of human potential, and approach to meaning-making that we have found crucial in developing our notions of teacher education at NCCAT. We think it imperative that we address each of these realms of meaning as a unique mode of human rationality that demands an equally specialized kind of educational sensitivity and social expression. This review is undertaken, in part, to highlight deficiencies in past research models of teacher education and to offer new insights into the knowledge and reasoning processes through which teacher renewal can be accomplished.

This more comprehensive model of teacher education, therefore, is composed of a series of decision-making realms designed to help teachers make sound judgments that promote consistency between the present situation, social norms, personal desires and feelings, social ideals, and effective individual action. Like a drama or theatrical production, such a decision-making structure provides teachers with a script that suggests general recommendations for decision making in the classroom. Unlike a drama or theatrical production, however, this decision-making structure can provide only generalized cues for producing a moral and just community, leaving to individual teacher/actors the task of determining the exact nature of their own teaching praxis.

This conception of teacher education implies a multidimensional theory of growth, development, and maturation. Reason is not a completed and changeless entity—it is not unchanging and unchangeable, as Plato thought. The process of discovering, constructing, and validating realms of human meaning-making is not a facile human activity. Problems are of many kinds; there is not one single method that may be designated as the only approach to problem solving. Many philosophers, however, attempted to do this. Bertrand Russell, for example, represents the mathematical approach to solving problems, while John Dewey prefers the scientific method. We maintain that the nature of the problem should determine which mode of inquiry should be used—mathematical, scientific, cultural, ethical, or one of personal aesthetical praxis. Accordingly, we speak of realms of meaning. Thus, our case study account of NCCAT's teacher renewal philosophy required a mapping of the realms of meaning, one in which the various possibilities of significant experience were charted and the domains of meaning distinguished and correlated.

Our NCCAT seminars are designed as a means by which teacher participants can reexamine, refine, and in some cases reconstruct their existing philosophical world views. To reexamine the personal aspects of one's conceptual structure, however, required time and probing self-examination. Our seminar week is designed to do just this. Our intent is to make philosophy and the philosophical odyssey part of one's day-to-day existence—just part of the ordinary, everyday process by which we grapple with the enduring problematic situations that confront us in our daily lives. By helping teachers to confront and manage the enduring problems of human existence, and by providing a conceptual framework for judging the adequacy of these solutions, philosophy gives us the means of mastery over our environments in ways that are true, morally justifiable, socially acceptable, and aesthetically pleasing. We hope that our NCCAT seminars help teacher participants to discover and refine this art of living completely and with a mastery that reflects their unique creative perspective and interests.

Such a creative approach to teacher education is designed to accomplish other aims as well. First, we hope that participants will come to view the development of a personal philosophy not as a fait accompli, but rather as a way to problem solve in their ongoing, day-to-day activities; second, we hope that this approach helps to remove maladaptive rigidity in their understanding of other human beings and cultures; and third, we hope that such an approach will result in a deepening appreciation for the unity and common nature that all peoples of all nations and races share. The psychological underpinning for engaging in such a philosophical odyssey is trust—a kind of supportive and trustful environment must be provided wherein individuals are free to explore the changing knowledge of the physical universe, the changing cultural contexts of our communities, the changing priorities in social ideals, and changing insights into how to integrate these new understandings into their current life plans.

Our own continuing research at the North Carolina Center for the Advancement of Teaching has led us to a number of conclusions and observations about different interpretation and ordering of these various disciplinary realms. It is beyond the scope of this chapter to articulate any detailed exposition of this research, but the reader should consult our previous publications for an in-depth treatment of this model.

Sensory Experience: The Touchstone of NCCAT Seminars

An initial caveat: Our approach to understanding in these various realms of human cognition rests on a conviction that the mind is dependent, to a large degree, on the body as the source or "raw material" of its cognitive processes. According to this view, the first acts of human cognition involve *perceiving* an object, forming a *percept* or phantasm (a cognitive representation of an object), and later extracting the essence (or universal) from the percept to form a *concept*. Common sensory experiences, therefore, form the foundation upon which all human rationality is established. It is simply the result of having a body with sense organs and motor capacities. These sensory experiences are nonreflective, physiologically based, and untaught. All our subsequent cognitive activity is simply filtered through or grafted onto the sensory knowledge base, especially our scientific knowledge base and sociocultural understandings.

It is in recognition of this pivotal role that sensory knowledge plays in all further cognitive development and reflection that we plan a rich sensory experiential component as a regular part of our NCCAT seminars. In "Why Wilderness," seminar participants sleep in the forest for three nights without the benefit of tents. In "Turners and Burners: The Folk Potters of North Carolina," the teachers learn how to throw pottery themselves and then travel to the actual craftshops of renowned North Carolinian potters. A rich sensory experiential component does two things: first, it provides a common experience from which all further realms can draw for seminar discussion; and second, these journeys of discovery and new experience symbolize the intellectual quest and personal renewal we hope will occur during the seminar week. This heightened sensory awareness is complemented by outstanding meals, live plants in every room, delightful musical entertainment, dramatic productions, art activities, film, exercise and nature walks, and so on. A clean and quiet seminar environment caters to the senses and forms the core of our seminar philosophy. At its higher and more pleasureful state, the development and refinement of our general sensory faculties open us to the wonder and delight of being alive.

Teacher Renewal as Skills Development

The first component of our approach to teacher education is the attempt to make clear the meaning of one's sensory experiences. This skills enhancement phase embodies three basic modes of knowing: the scientific method, logical analysis, and the establishment of a technical skill. Any comprehensive model of teacher education should focus equally on these modes of cognition, and we have found these various ways of knowing useful in designing our NCCAT seminars.

The Scientific Method

Let us begin by considering what science can and cannot do and its proper scope and function. The sciences study physical and social phenomena in order to arrive at an accurate picture of them. Empirical science is a mode of inquiry designed to solve situationally specific problems. The primary scientific concern is to understand and control nature as a resource, and to use it efficiently through the development of predictable technological systems. Scientific experimentation attempts to understand how things behave; it may be concerned with the movement of the heavenly bodies, the inner workings of the atom, physiological processes, social movements, or human behavior. What is the utility of scientific knowledge? Francis Bacon answered that question by saying that science gives us power. It enables us to exercise a certain degree of mastery or control over the physical and social phenomena of the world in which we live. Thus, science aims to provide an understanding of the nature of reality—this is the grounding of scientific knowledge. The scientific method aims to generate reliable information that can be independently known apart from particular human interests, values, purposes, and hopes. This ideal of objectivity to which the sciences aspire, however, is shaped by the prior perspective provided by sensory experience.

The facts or the circumstantial data that we accept at any particular historical juncture regarding the structures, the situation, and/or the processes of any particular seminar topic form the structure upon which we build our seminar decision making. Often this more factual information is sent to the seminar participants in the form of pre-seminar reading.

Logical Analysis

The first Center fellows pinpointed their efforts on the issue of logic and thinking skills. Their concerns shaped and focused the attention of the staff in subsequent NCCAT meetings. Discussions in staff circles during the last half of 1987 led, for instance, to a statement entitled "A Taxonomy of NCCAT Thinking Skills," which included items such as listening for the structure of an argument; asking for clarification of assertions; and synthesizing and comparing diverging viewpoints. This statement stands as a mute but powerful testimony to a principal preoccupation of the Center practitioners after only a year of Center operation. Communicating one's point of view—precisely, clearly, and persuasively—was rightly judged to be the necessary prerequisite of any real dialogue or discussion format. Given the rather orthodox Adlerian text-driven seminar model that formed the inspiration for the original pilot programs, it is not surprising that an early emphasis was on developing these skills in grammar, logic, and rhetoric.

Technical Skills Development

The technical skills aspect of teacher education rests on three important assumptions—that discrete pedagogical skills can be identified; that the skills can be transmitted to prospective practitioners; and that they can be appropriately drawn upon in practice to improve teacher performance (Kennedy, 1987, p. 155). Teacher practitioners need skills as do other professionals. In a recent study, Mary Kennedy of Michigan State University found that the complete exclusion of technical skills training from programs of engineering education left engineers completely unprepared for professional practice (Kennedy, 1987, p. 130). Likewise, emphasis on technical skills development was deemed to be an essential component to facilitate teacher renewal. Thus, almost every one of our NCCAT seminars has a decidedly technical component—how to fish, how to measure water flow, how to play a musical instrument, how to measure solar energy and direction, and so forth.

Teacher Renewal as Sociocultural Expression

The second component of the NCCAT approach to teacher education is the attempt to provide an accounting for the social significance of the scientific facts, logical assertions, and technical skills generated in the skills development realm. The immediate interest we have as human beings is that we live in a world and we must cope with it—some facts, logical assertions, and technical skills help us; some do not. The cultural realm provides a way of interpreting the facts and helping us to understand their cultural significance.

Even though the facts are what they are, not all facts are equally significant. What establishes the importance of some facts and what guides our interest in them is their relevance to the problems we encounter in our everyday lives. Thus, a necessary part of any NCCAT seminar is that we not only have an interest in the facts concerning a particular topic, but also have a special desire to know what these facts mean in terms of our own particular cultural environments.

Another function of this cultural realm within our NCCAT seminars is that it allows for the development of strong bonds of collegiality. Collegiality is enhanced when people engage in joint action, when they share experiences and understand one another. Again, the necessary condition for such communication is trust. For this to occur, the teachers must have real opportunities to enter into group seminar discussions and express freely their own beliefs. At the same time, they must feel confident enough to challenge constructively what others have to say. Although such a vision dramatically conflicts with the present-day realities of our American ethic of competitive capitalism, it does provide the beginnings of an alternative world view.

Given these assumptions, cultural inquiry seeks situational insights and meanings. Special emphasis is placed on the importance of communication and meaning-making that must be continually redefined via intersubjective meanings. The mountain that is reality can be seen from an enormous range of perspectives, each of which, although incomplete, gives a partial view. Good decision making requires that all perspectives be heard and evaluated.

Teacher Renewal as Moral Decision Making

The first two realms of decision making can help us determine only "What appears to be the case?" and "What are the facts?" in our present physical and social environment. They cannot help us decide questions of value. The conduct of human life and the organization of human society depend on our answers to such questions as what should happiness consist of, what ought our social obligations be, what form of government is most just, what constitutes the common good of society, what freedom should we have, and so on. Not one of these questions, which involve a discussion of right or wrong, can be answered by science or cultural sociology. It is social ethics, not science, that helps us to choose the social ideals that befit our human nature. Each kind of knowledge answers questions that the other cannot answer, and that is why each is useful in a different way.

The third aspect of what we see as the NCCAT philosophy of teacher education is something we loosely refer to as the social ideals component. During this stage, we observe that seminar participants begin to construct a system of social ideals. The construction of such a system of social ideals forces the teachers to reflect on their own most basic needs and those of other cultural groups that form the world community. What they discover is that what is really good and most basic for themselves is good in exactly the same sense for every other human being, because what is really good is what satisfies the desires and needs inherent in human nature. We are all members of the same biological species, and it is upon this base that we claim fundamental human rights from our political systems as members of the human species. The rational and just identification and implementation of social ideals is the connecting link between ethical and political decision making, and forms the substructure of social ethics (Adler, 1971).

The explication and justification of social ideals is one of the prime philosophical tasks of a good NCCAT seminar. Through a process of creative imaging, an idealized future community is conceptualized. From the director's opening seminar commentary to the Saturday morning group oral evaluation session, visions and metaphorical insights into the workings of a more moral and harmonious social order are kept prominent on the seminar agenda. By helping seminar participants to eliminate either impractical utopian dreams or clearly unethical alternatives, the seminar framework helps individuals to determine which choices are available to them. The seminar participants are left with a range of ethically viable alternatives that unite all human beings in a single moral community and unite us as members of the human species. It is from these common elements that we derive our notions of basic human rights and the common good, upon whose fulfillment rest the foundations for our global conceptions of the moral community.

These NCCAT seminar discussions come about through the process of active inquiry. In the process of identifying and describing different conceptual constellations and world views, one has already moved beyond narrow social adjustment. At this point, one becomes self-reflective about one's beliefs and commitments, and begins to form social ideals about visions beyond one's own cultural context. Our claim is that there is a metalevel context of decision making that transcends these heretofore discrete paradigm sets; its aim is to generate discussions about the global nature of the moral community.

Teacher Renewal as Aesthetic Praxis

The fourth component of NCCAT's approach to teacher education is aesthetic praxis. Seminar participants quickly concede that life in any culture always seems to fall short of the ideals to which the culture aspires. They begin then to engage in a diagnosis of their culture's shortcomings, as measured by the discrepancy between common social ideals and their culture's present condition. At the same time, they begin to devise an action plan to remediate identified deficiencies and shortcomings.

A policy for coping with or overcoming the discrepancy between the ideal and the actual is uniquely individual. During this phase, participants consider only the means that the individual—a single human being—ought to employ to achieve the good life for him- or herself. As the seminar process continues the individual is asked to consider what one should do within an is-ought framework. The object of rationality in this realm is to achieve some kind of internal consistency between the facts, norms, feelings, social ideals, and one's present and future planned social action and behavior.

Obligations are concerned with what one thinks one ought to act and feel or is expected to act and feel in terms of one's present cultural group. Expectations deal with how others (i.e., the idealized moral community) expect one to act and feel, based on common ethical criteria. The tension between these two realms provides the skeleton of the decision-making structure within which one operates. If the decision-making process is successful, the individual should be able to generate a well-developed ethical framework for personal decision making, which would include a variety of choices. The last day of the NCCAT seminar is typically when we allow time (perhaps the entire day) for the participants to imagine, create, and share with the group their own individual responses to the seminar themes. Sometimes their diagnosis will be optimistic, and their praxis will be a forward-looking plan of action. Sometimes their diagnosis will be pessimistic, and the aim of their personal praxis will be minor adjustments or a small-scale amelioration (i.e., doing as well as possible given the particular situation that one confronts).

If one is successful in implementing personal praxis, the result is what we have observed here at NCCAT as a feeling of transcendence. This achievement, the level of aesthetic praxis, is accompanied by the sheer delight that a human organism experiences having achieved consistency between personal feelings, cultural interests, social ideals, and appropriate social action. With practice, humans develop internal cognitive skills that enable them to achieve an internal consistency in their daily decisions and judgments. Individuals learn how to provide both the internal space needed for self-reflection and the external space needed for democratically convened social groupings. As these social habits become more integrated, they also become more complex. As individuals mature and become more adept at the process of decision making, they gain new and more complex decision-making skills—skills that help them decide what is needed to achieve the good life for themselves and their communities.

However, while there is a consensus on how best to derive universal social ideals and on the centrality that these social ideals should play in our lives, there is no consensus on how to best express these ideals in one's own life and behavior. Decision making in this realm is more of an art. It involves improvisation and an appraisal of the fit between one's own personal situation and the world community. Reason is central, but intuition and feeling play a role. To be right in the realm of aesthetic praxis is to have ethically justified policies, but also to have a praxis that is emotionally satisfying as well as aesthetically suitable.

The realm of aesthetic praxis is the commitment one must make with one's life to actualize one's chosen philosophy; it is a commitment and a praxis that will never be complete or perfected. Although nature and social ideals dictate the range of choices in any given situation, the way in which we configure and arrange our choices offers endless opportunities for creative improvisation. The realm of aesthetic praxis is, at its best, an exercise in intelligent, creative improvisation. In the best sense of the word, it should be for teachers a kind of playful jazz session. Its primary function, however, is more serious—that is, to enable us to make our philosophy of life a matter of choice, rather than of habit or dogmatic compliance.

This research leads one to conclude that there is a direct connection between teacher renewal and school reform. Programs of teacher education need to be individualized enough to allow for the myriad renewal needs of their participants. However, this approach assumes that if we do our teacher renewal jobs well, the issue of school reform will take care of itself. Democratic models of school reform depend on the existence of a knowledgeable, technically proficient, morally adept, culturally astute, aesthetically sensitive, and politically empowered teaching force. Renewed teachers can bring about reform to deficient and dysfunctional school structures.

Conclusion

This thematic overview of the history of teacher education in America reconfirmed something that we have become increasingly aware of here at NCCAT—that there are crucial differences between programs of teacher education based on a concept of teacher reform and those based on a concept of teacher renewal. Although our process of curriculum development at NCCAT has been episodic, fragmentary, and incomplete, its grounding in a solid philosophical justification as well as a democratic mode of decision making has functioned to keep the process experimental, self-renewing, and self-actualizing. It was only in retrospect that we began to identify the various components that were emerging in our NCCAT seminars and to relate them to a larger, more comprehensive view of a teacher renewal philosophy. Our work on these themes continues, too.

References

Adler, M. (1971). *The commonsense of politics.* New York: Holt, Rinehart and Winston.
Blatz, W. (1944). *Understanding the young child.* New York: William Morrow.
Bolin, F., & Falk, J. (1987). *Teacher renewal: Professional issues, personal choices.* New York: Teachers College Press.
Boyce, A. C. (1915). *Methods for measuring teachers' efficiency.* 14th yearbook of the National Society for the Study of Education, Part II. Chicago: University of Chicago Press.
Bunzel, J. (Ed.). (1985). *Challenge to American schools: The case for standards and values.* New York: Oxford University Press.
Burke, P. J. (1987). *Teacher development: Induction, renewal, and redirection.* New York: Falmer Press.
Charters, W. W., & Waples, D. (1929). *The Commonwealth teacher training study.* New York: Commonwealth Fund.
Cooley, C. H. (1909). *Social organization: A study of the larger mind.* New York: Schocken Books.

Cooley, W. W. (1989). *An evaluation of the North Carolina Center for the Advancement of Teaching*. Pittsburgh: University of Pittsburgh.
Cuban, L. (1984). *How teachers taught: Constancy and change in American classrooms, 1890-1980*. New York: Longman.
Dewey, J. (1939). The problem of freedom. In *Freedom and culture* (pp. 3-23). New York: Capricorn Books.
Dickson, G. E., Saxe, R. W., et al. (1973). *Partners for educational reform and renewal*. Berkeley: McCutchan.
Habermas, J. (1971). *Knowledge and human interests*. Boston: Beacon Press.
Habermas, J. (1973). *Theory and practice*. Boston: Beacon Press.
Iowa Child Welfare Research Station, University of Iowa. (1933). *Pioneering in child welfare: A history of the Iowa Welfare Research Station*. Iowa City: University of Iowa.
Iowa Child Welfare Research Station, University of Iowa. (1967). *Institute of child behavior and development: Fifty years of research, 1917-1967*. Iowa City: University of Iowa.
Kennedy, M. M. (1987). Inexact sciences: Professional education and the development of expertise. In E. Z. Rothkopf (Ed.), *New research in education* (pp. 133-167). Washington, DC: American Educational Research Association.
McPherson, R. B. (1990, January). *The teacher as student: Lessons for leaders*. Paper presented at the North Carolina ASCD Conference, Pinehurst.
McPherson, R. B., Crowson, R. L., & Pitner, N. J. (1986). *Managing uncertainty: Administrative theory and practice in education*. Columbus, OH: Merrill.
Mann, H. (1853). *A few thoughts on the powers and duties of women*. Syracuse: Hall, Mills.
Mattingly, P. (1975). *The classless profession: American schoolmen in the nineteenth century*. New York: New York University Press.
Mead, G. H. (1934). *Mind, self, and society*. Chicago: University of Chicago Press.
Melder, K. (1977). Mask of oppression: The female seminary movement in the United States. *New York History, 16*, 260-279.
Nash, P. (1975). A humanistic approach to performance-based teacher education. In R. A. Smith (Ed.), *Regaining educational leadership: Critical essays on PBTE/CBTE, behavioral objectives and accountability* (pp. 186-201). New York: John Wiley.
Park, R. E., & Burgess, E. W. (1921). *Introduction to the science of sociology*. Chicago: University of Chicago Press.
Ryan, K. (1975). *Teacher education*. 74th yearbook of the National Society for the Study of Education, Part II. Chicago: University of Chicago Press.
Schiffer, J. (1980). *School renewal through staff development*. New York: Teachers College Press.
Shea, C. M. (1975). *Horace Mann, the Boston Associates, and the feminization of the common schools*. Unpublished paper, Department of Educational Policy Studies, University of Illinois, Champaign.
Shea, C. M., & McPherson, R. B. (1990, April). *Practitioner-generated theory:*

The discovery of an aesthetic level to adult education. Paper presented at the American Educational Research Association, Boston.

Shea, C. M., & McPherson, R. B. (forthcoming). *Practitioner-generated theory: The discovery of an aesthetic level to adult education.*

Shea, C. M., et al. (1989). *The new servants of power: A critique of the 1980's school reform movement.* New York: Praeger.

Sherman, M. (1938). *Mental conflicts and personality.* New York: Longmans, Green.

Spring, J. (1986). *The American school, 1642-1985.* New York: Longman.

Travers, R. M. (1983). *How research has changed American schools, A history from 1840 to the present.* Kalamazoo, MI: Mythos Press.

Webb, R., & Ashton, P. T. (1979). Teacher motivation and the conditions of teaching: A call for ecological reform. In S. Walker & L. Barton (Eds.), *Changing policies, changing teachers: New directions for schooling?* (pp. 22-40). Philadelphia: Open University Press.

White House Conference on Child Health and Protection, Report of the Committee on the Infant and Preschool Child, J. E. Anderson (chair). (1936). *The young child in the home, A survey of three thousand American families.* New York: D. Appleton.

Chapter 2

Why North Carolina?: The Early History of a Teacher Renewal Effort

DIANE K. HOFFBAUER

I became involved in writing about the Center for a number of reasons. I had spent many years in the educational systems of Minnesota, a state known for its innovative educational programs. My teaching in New York State and Thailand over a decade ago presented new challenges to me. I moved to North Carolina in the early 1980s and looked for a teaching position that would offer similar challenge and interest. My initial jobs in migrant education, substitute teaching, and community college instruction provided me with the opportunity to see many teachers, schools, and students in trouble. Dropout rates were high, teacher morale was low, and I did not get a real sense of community concern about education, teachers, and schools in North Carolina.

During this period I bagan to read the newspaper reports of Governor James Hunt's Commission of Education for Economic Growth and the preliminary work toward the establishment of a teacher center. It seemed to be a fresh and innovative concept that would be enacted for the benefit of the group for whom I was most concerned—teachers. I had by then enrolled in a doctoral program in education at the University of South Carolina and was working at Western Carolina University (WCU) in Cullowhee, North Carolina, where NCCAT was being established. With the encouragement of my graduate professors, I reviewed unpublished letters, speeches, notes, reports, and meeting minutes, as well as newspaper articles and other published records and reports, to document the establishment and early growth of this new organization.

The Genesis of an Idea

The official planning for the multimillion dollar North Carolina Center for the Advancement of Teaching was initiated in October

1984. In an era of budget cuts and standardized curriculum, how and why did such a project come to pass in a state traditionally recognized for low graduation and literacy rates, below average test scores, and poor teacher morale? Documents and interviews with key figures from the past 20 years provide a window for viewing the development of this Center and the strong commitment to improve education in North Carolina by political leaders, business representatives, and educators. As a result of substantial planning by these leaders, a unique and invigorating approach to rewarding and renewing outstanding teachers was created.

Although a number of educational, social, and political circumstances led to the development of the Center, the support of the governor of North Carolina at that time, James B. Hunt, Jr., was surely the most critical. Since his tenure in office began in 1977, Governor Hunt was directly involved in supporting a number of important educational programs. The North Carolina Writing Project and the Principals' Institute serve teachers and administrators of the state's schools. The Community Schools Program and the Adopt-a-School Program involved the people of North Carolina with their schools. The Governor's School for the state's specially talented, the North Carolina School of Science and Mathematics, a competency testing and remediation program, more stringent graduation requirements, and the North Carolina Scholars program were among initiatives aimed at improving student achievement. Many other programs that encompass school discipline, dropout prevention, students with special needs, vocational education, and a state salary schedule/benefits for teachers were also implemented (Owen, 1984a).

Improving schools was especially critical to North Carolina for a number of reasons. In the 1970s primary students in the state were scoring below the national average in reading, the high school dropout rate was over 30 percent, and more than 10 percent failed the reading or mathematics component of the Competency Testing Program when it was first implemented in 1978 (North Carolina Commission on Education for Economic Growth, 1984). Teachers were becoming increasingly dismayed with the low salaries and poor working conditions of the schools.

The awakening of the national education reform movement during the mid-1980s provided motivation for much-needed improvements in schools and in the field of professional teacher development. *A Nation at Risk: The Imperative for Educational Reform* (National Commission on Excellence in Education, 1983) was one of many reports that provided recommendations for local, state, national, and international reform and innovation. Concurrently, North Carolina endeavored to become an economic leader in the Southeast. Business, political, and education leaders such as James Hunt recognized that for North Carolina to be an economic power, the people needed to be educated to produce, to invent, and to compete—to do the kinds of work and to solve the kinds of problems the remainder of this century and the next century will produce. In 1981, Hunt and his senior advisor, Elizabeth (Betty) Owen, began to discuss these educational issues to decide which ones Hunt would focus on during his second administration. Owen, a veteran teacher of 25 years with a history of commitment to education through her teaching, consulting, school board involvement, and state-level work throughout the country, had assisted Hunt in his educational endeavors almost 10 years earlier while he was serving as North Carolina's lieutenant governor. She remembers the discussions that were the prelude to the development of NCCAT: "Of all the education reforms that had been debated and discussed, making significant changes on behalf of teachers and the teaching profession seemed to hold the most promise" (personal communication, March 17, 1988).

Education Commission of the States

As part of his interest in strengthening the public schools and in helping them serve as a vehicle for general economic growth in North Carolina, in 1982–1983 Hunt chaired the Education Commission of the States, a nonprofit, nationwide educational compact. The primary purpose of the Commission is to help governors, state legislators, state education officials, and others develop policies to improve the quality of education at all levels. Hunt immediately created the Task Force on Education for Economic Growth, which he chaired with Frank Cary of IBM and Governor Pierre duPont of Delaware. Following its first meeting in February 1983, the Task Force served as an avenue for governors, business leaders, and educators to build an action plan. In its 1983 report, *Action for Excellence: A Comprehensive Plan to Improve Our Nation's Schools*, the Task Force emphasized the importance of education to a strong national economy and recommended that states develop plans for improving public education (Task Force on Education, 1983).

North Carolina Commission on Education for Economic Growth

Hunt created the North Carolina Commission on Education for Economic Growth (NCCEEG) in October 1983. Comprising 50 leaders representing business, education, government, parents, students, and the media, the Commission appraised education in North Carolina and presented recommendations for ensuring economic growth and prosperity. These recommendations included planning for excellence, building partnerships (especially with business), marshalling resources, enhancing the teaching profession, strengthening academic programs, providing quality assurance in education, improving leadership and management in schools, and better serving the unserved and underserved student (NCCEEG, 1984).

As part of its appraisal, the Commission held four public hearings in North Carolina in 1984 in an effort to gain public input on how to improve the quality of education in the state. Owen said:

> Over and over again people appeared at the public hearings to underscore their concerns about schools and particularly about teachers. We determined that our most important task was to make teaching a more attractive profession. We wanted to strengthen, renew, and reward teachers in completely new ways. (personal communication, March 17, 1988)

Jean Powell, a high school English teacher and the 1983–1984 North Carolina Teacher of the Year from Clinton, was invited to speak by the governor's office at the first of these public hearings. In responding to a quote by James Garfield, "I am not willing that this discussion should close without mention of the value of a true teacher. Give me a log hut, with only a simple bench, Mark Hopkins on one end and I on the other, and you may have all the buildings, apparatus and libraries without him," Powell (1983) stated:

> I teach in a public high school more than 100 years later. . . . We not only are expected to educate everybody, but also we are expected to provide social services, and act as surrogate parent, nurse, nutritionist, sex counselor, and policeman. Suffice it to say that no matter how dedicated, even inspirational I am, that log hut with a simple bench just won't cut it. Those 150 students I see each day would spend a lot of time waiting in line to get on the other end of that bench.
>
> So—what will make that environment more productive for my students? How will the environment attract and retain the best teachers? . . . To attract and retain the best in education, we must find a way to enhance the teacher's sense of self-worth, . . . pride of accomplishment, and . . . enthusiasm. We have a governor's school for gifted students. Why not something similar for teachers? We

don't need more educational methodology or the latest curriculum fads. We'd like to study the "real stuff." What about going to summer school for 1 or 2 weeks, or even 4 to 6 weeks, to study some of the great books: Plato, Homer, Virgil, Shakespeare, and others? Include the opportunity to visit an art gallery, see live performances of Shakespeare's plays along with videotapes and films, with outside reading and even writing critical commentaries. If that kind of learning experience doesn't turn on teachers of the humanities, I don't know what will. That excitement will be communicated to students. Furthermore, being a student will give a teacher a renewed perspective of the student's role.

The testimony from Powell suggested that North Carolina needed to do something unique in the field of education. The comments were timely as Hunt and the education leaders of North Carolina searched for creative strategies for continuing to improve the educational climate of the state, especially teacher compensation, and they helped to influence the Commission to see that "enhancing the teaching profession" and the idea of a special teacher center were indeed an important focus. With Hunt's determination to make North Carolina responsive to innovative educational enterprises, NCCAT quickly developed into a much larger entity than Powell's original idea of a teacher "summer school."

On April 5, 1984, Hunt presented *Education for Economic Growth: An Action Plan for North Carolina* (NCCEEG, 1984) at the Raleigh Civic Center to hundreds of interested educators, community members, and representatives of business and industry. The report had one overwhelming theme, namely, raised expectations for what the schools must and could accomplish. One recommendation read:

> Express a high regard for teachers and for teaching in North Carolina by improving all the conditions of the profession in our state: teacher recruitment, training, certification, pay, career incentives and the teaching environment. (p. 24)

Seven strategies for guaranteeing the success of this particular recommendation were discussed. The concept of a teacher center emerged as the third strategy.

> The General Assembly, the State Board of Education, and the University of North Carolina Board of Governors should establish a Center for the Advancement of Teaching—an institute to provide outstanding teachers with an opportunity to study the sciences and

humanities and consider and recommend better ways of teaching young people. (p. 24)

Educators across the state soon became aware that Hunt valued rewarding the hard work and dedication of good teachers and the importance of making excellent teaching a pleasure. Within the next few weeks, Hunt received letters and resolutions of overwhelming support from business leaders, superintendents, educators, the North Carolina Association of Educators (NCAE), the North Carolina Association of School Administrators, and other organizations. One who wrote urged the political leaders of the state to begin the implementation of the recommendations immediately (Jackson, 1984). Soon Owen from the governor's office and Donald J. Stedman, Associate Vice President for Academic Affairs, University of North Carolina, embarked on planning that would make the Center an integral part of North Carolina's response to the national challenge for the improvement of public education.

The Conception of the Center's Mission

Hunt recognized that the Center would provide both short- and long-term, in-residence learning and study opportunities in advanced topics and issues related to teaching and education for selected mid-career outstanding teachers. Teachers would pursue interdisciplinary or thematic approaches to topics and issues related to teaching and education. The Center was designed to have regional, statewide, and national impact, and would serve as a model for similar enrichment programs across the country (Owen, 1984c; B. Owen, personal communication, March 17, 1988).

Knowing the successful implementation of such an idea would revolve around funding, Hunt prepared a budget recommendation for the June 1984 short session of the North Carolina General Assembly. The request for $100,000 to establish a planning group for the Center was not funded because other activities recommended by Hunt's Commission held greater priority. With direction from Hunt, Owen began to look for alternative sources to fund this project (personal communication, March 17, 1988).

In 1983 the Appalachian Regional Commission (ARC) affirmed its support for improving education and training for the work force by revising its code to recognize the need for improvements in education that would raise the levels of both basic and employability skills, or that would address lifelong needs of Appalachian workers for retraining opportunities (ARC, 1983). In 1984 the ARC recognized the need for special technical assistance to further these changes. In July 1984 Owen submitted a proposal to the ARC to fund and locate the Center in western North Carolina (part of the Appalachian region) in an effort to create the atmosphere of a mountain retreat (Owen, 1984b). A number of chancellors from the 16-campus University of North Carolina system were interested in having the Center located at their institutions. H. F. Robinson, chancellor of Western Carolina University, staked a claim to the Center in a letter, dated April 2, 1984, to William Friday, president of the University of North Carolina (UNC). With more than a 10-year history of campaigning for and initiating improvements in education in western North Carolina, Robinson argued that this project was in line with his belief and actions that WCU should be the cradle of schooling for the mountain area. He was a long-time friend of Speaker of the House of Representatives Liston Ramsey, who was also from western North Carolina. They had worked together on a number of educational projects in the state. Soon Ramsey, Robinson, and other WCU administrators were engaged in informal preliminary discussions about a center for the advancement of teaching (H. F. Robinson, personal communication, February 18, 1988). The ARC then agreed to provide $150,000 assistance through September 1985 for the planning and establishment of such a center at WCU (ARC, 1984).

The Planning Committee, appointed by Governor Hunt, was composed of representatives from business, education, and government (Hunt, 1984a). They met for the first time in late 1984 and presented administrators from WCU with a draft concept paper. This document was one of the first attempts to put the vision of the Center into writing.

> The Center will provide both long-term and short-term in-residence learning and study opportunities for selected outstanding professional teachers. The objective of the Center will be to improve the effectiveness of teachers by providing them with opportunities to pursue, on an intensive basis, programs of study and activities at an advanced level to enhance their ability as teachers, lead to an enhancement of their status, and enable them to keep abreast of emerging concepts and technologies.
>
> The Center will provide the type of advanced educational opportunity outstanding teachers need and deserve. It will enhance their effectiveness as teachers and also will send to them a strong

signal that they are valued for their contributions as serious scholars and as leaders of our young people and our communities. (Owen, 1984c, pp. 1-2)

Although this initial concept paper concentrated on the recognition of teachers, an additional goal included the creating and placing of dynamic instructional leaders in North Carolina schools. Succeeding discussions centered around the necessity for a statewide focus for locating both participants and resources and for emphasizing the importance of excellence; the selection process would be competitive and involve outstanding teachers. Minutes from the November 29, 1984, meeting of the Planning Committee reveal that the members were adamant that although the Center would be part of the reward structure for teachers, it would not be part of the traditional form of staff development (where teachers attended for credit) and would not be involved with the licensing or credentialing of teachers in any manner. They also considered the importance of acknowledging the Center's alumni and did not want the teachers' first involvement with the Center to be conclusive. The role and value of evaluation first surfaced during this preliminary meeting and would be discussed during many subsequent planning sessions.

Aware that he was soon to leave office, in December 1984 Governor Hunt made a final push for education reform by proposing an ambitious $16.8 billion state budget for 1985-1987 (Leland, 1984). The emphasis of the budget continued to be on strengthening the state's economy through improvements in education, and included was $2.5 million for the creation of the Center for the Advancement of Teaching over the next two years (Hunt, 1984b). The new governor, Jim Martin, voiced support for the development of the Center in his March 1, 1985, State of the State address, but at a lowered funding level. Although confrontation was expected in the General Assembly over the budget differences, it did not happen, and the funding requested by Hunt was secured.

As the planning of the Center progressed throughout the winter of 1985, one unresolved question that sparked debate involved the determination of a permanent location. Although the ARC had agreed in its planning grant to locate the Center at WCU, there was no formal legislation in place to ensure that placement, and administrators from other institutions continued to argue the most appropriate site. The Planning Committee began to develop a governance plan for the Center, the 1985 summer pilot programs, and future budgets. In addition, members began to research other institutes and centers throughout the United States (such as the Aspen Institute's Wye Faculty Seminars) that could serve as models for the Center's development. Speakers from various organizations and institutions, such as the North Carolina Humanities Committee, met with the Planning Committee to voice their support and offer suggestions. A review of the minutes of these planning sessions shows that these meetings served to articulate the needs for the Center and laid the groundwork for the work plan that would provide direction for developing and implementing a model of operation.

Facilities Development

After extensive research and site visitation, the Facility Planning and Site Alternatives Work Group members presented recommendations to the Planning Committee regarding meeting rooms, scheduling, and audiovisual equipment at the May 7-8, 1985, meeting in Asheville. It was also suggested that the Center construct a building for potential hotel training business, plan for some separation of participant groups, and decide on programming formats and desired environments before designing a core facility. If the planners had listened carefully to this report, they would have heard the suggestion for a large, multipurpose center. Since some members appeared not to have heard this, the facility size was a surprise, and subsequently a matter of controversy. It had been suggested that WCU retain responsibility for facilities governance; as a result it appeared to some members that WCU staff viewed the building as an expansion of their own institution and did not recognize the Center as a separate state education entity governed by the University of North Carolina.

The Planning Committee met for the seventh and final time in August 1985 to assess the first three pilot summer programs, which had recently been completed, and to approve the final report for the ARC. In accordance with the grant agreement with the governor's office, the report summarized the Planning Committee's findings and recommendations for the Center. The report would continue to serve as a useful, flexible framework for institutionalizing the Center (Report and Recommendations of the Planning Committee, 1985).

Reward, Renewal, Retention

From the initial planning meetings, key concepts and themes emerged that focused on the rewarding of teachers and the development of a teacher center. Hunt stated clearly in his April 1984 report that he intended to "reward hard work and dedication" (NCCEEG, 1984). "Renewal," "reward," and "intellectual stimulation" appeared in documents and concept papers as the Planning Committee members endeavored to formalize the philosophy and direction of the Center. Project director Gurney Chambers discussed the need to keep good teachers in the classroom, the need to refresh and renew the self-worth of teachers, and the need for teachers to have intellectually stimulating experiences. At a speech to the participants of the first pilot seminar in 1985, Chambers publicly used the succinct phrase "renewal, reward, and retention" to describe the purpose and philosophy of the Center (personal communication, June 26, 1988). The NCCAT staff, dedicated to the advancement of teaching as an art and a profession, extended this philosophy as they developed the critical programming component.

Programming Alternatives and Decisions

The programming for the Center was the most critical of all the tasks. Planners got direct input from teachers regarding participant selection, programming alternatives, and possible constraints. The Program Planning and Research Work Group held four meetings across the state during February 1985 to discuss a variety of program models and strategies. Robert Stoltz, WCU's Vice Chancellor for Academic Affairs and project coordinator, and Martha McKinney, his assistant, were attentive to the teachers' responses and recognized that the Center concept was receiving broad-based support among those in attendance. This intense grass-roots aspect of the development proved to be significant in defining the philosophy and goals of the Center and in establishing a strong political base as teachers were encouraged to serve as technical advisors for the duration of the planning period. Stoltz remembers these meetings.

> One of the things we did not know was the extent to which the vision that Jean Powell had was shared by other teachers. When we talked to other teachers we found there was much enthusiasm for the idea. Things that we encountered spontaneously from the first meeting we checked with the other groups . . . we had very little trouble getting responses from the teachers. (personal communication, March 10, 1988)

A teacher from a small mountain town commented in a February 1985 letter to Stoltz that "North Carolina teachers will be moving a step closer to being treated as professionals as the center goes into operation. . . . The experience of selection should above all be the honor which is intended."

Additional meetings were held with other clientele groups, including university and college deans, school administrators and principals, and organizations such as the North Carolina Association of Educators (NCAE), to request advice and feedback regarding the programming plans (Stoltz & McKinney, 1985a). According to Stoltz, no direct, formal opposition to the Center was voiced during these state meetings, though some doubts and questions did surface concerning the funding level, the role of another "center" in North Carolina, and whether the reward for teachers should perhaps be a direct salary increase rather than a special program. Others did not understand the proposed Center's concept and questioned whether the state needed "another teacher training institution" (R. Stoltz, personal communication, March 10, 1988). Even Planning Committee members such as J. Robinson remembered thinking the idea of the Center was superb, but wondered who would fund such an expensive and first-class project. He said, "I underestimated the General Assembly's willingness to make this kind of investment" (personal communication, March 18, 1988).

The Summer Pilot Programs

Three key components for programming that had been identified in initial concept papers began to serve as a structure for program planning and the development of the pilot seminars to be offered during July 1985 (Stoltz & McKinney, 1985a):

1. Exposure of teachers to key thinkers in both formal and informal settings
2. Time for independent study, reading, and reflection
3. Leisure time, field trips, and time for interaction with peers

The pilot programs for the first 51 teachers were prepared using contacts that McKinney and other planners had made through their various visits to other institutes and programs around the country. In an effort to have a cross-section of educators, the selection process took into consideration such factors as gender, race, age, subject taught, geographical location of home school, date of application, and reasons for applying (Stoltz & McKinney, 1985a).

The first program, "New Frontiers in Teaching and Learning," an extended weekend seminar, was developed by Bruce Stewart, headmaster of the Abington Friends Schools in Pennsylvania and a member of the Planning Committee. Stewart previously had worked with former governor Terry Sanford in the early planning of the North Carolina School of Science and Mathematics and the North Carolina School of the Arts. Stewart contracted Mel Levine, noted researcher and chief of the Division of Ambulatory Pediatrics at Boston Children's Hospital, who discussed the implications of the newest research neurology and child development for classroom instruction. Other presenters included Douglas List from McKinsey and Company, who led a discussion on excellence principles and organizational theories that might be used in public education, and educational historian Diane Ravitch, who addressed the crisis in American education and the future of education (Stoltz & McKinney, 1985b).

A second seminar, "Citizenship, Education, and Democracy," was coordinated by Sherry Magill, Executive Director of the Wye Faculty Seminar, a program for the faculty of small liberal arts colleges patterned after the Aspen Institute. Each day of this seminar was structured around a particular theme, including "Our Founding Faiths," "The State: Imperative and Idea," "Dissent and Civil Disobedience," "Good Leaders and Effective Leadership," and "Education for the Polity." A number of presenters were involved, including Graham Martin, former U.S. ambassador to South Vietnam (Stoltz & McKinney, 1985b).

The third and final program, a seminar entitled "Powers of Technology/Powers of Culture," was coordinated by Brent Glass, Director of the North Carolina Humanities Committee, and a quietly powerful member of the Planning Committee. At the suggestions of the teachers who helped plan this seminar, the program emphasized the exchange of ideas among participants more than formal presentations. Through carefully selected readings such as *Brave New World*, "The Grand Inquisitor," *The Tempest*, and selections from Blake and Plato, discussions moderated by guest scholars provided teachers a chance to explore the past and future goals of technology in shaping Western civilization (Stoltz & McKinney, 1985b).

Although no major philosophical changes occurred in the 1986 programming, more adequate planning time enabled NCCAT staff members to pursue the development of seminars that would be inspirational to teachers and would reinforce the idea that teachers had value. As recommended in the 1985 evaluations, the independent research project component was eliminated and the schedule was changed to ensure that the participants adequate time for recreational activities, informal discourse, and private pursuits. A number of the presenters and program coordinators from the 1985 pilots were once again contracted, and additional themes and formats were explored (Bickel & Cooley, 1985).

The first seminar, an extended weekend entitled "Discovery," included Paul MacCready, recognized for his human- and solar-powered flying vehicles. James Gifford, Associate Professor of Community and Family Medicine at Duke University, discussed medical discoveries as a framework for exploring the nature of creativity in the classroom. The second seminar, week-long and entitled "Conflict and Compromise: American Foreign Policy through the Eyes of a Statesman," included Dean Rusk and former U.S. ambassadors Martin Hillenbrand and Graham Martin for an examination of U.S. foreign policy. The third seminar, also week-long and entitled "Leadership, Creativity, and Change," brought together Edward O'Neil, Assistant Dean of the UNC-Chapel Hill School of Dentistry and former program director of the W. K. Kellogg Foundation's National Leadership Program, and Frank McNutt, Assistant Dean of Residential Life at Duke University (Bickel, 1986).

Evaluation played a critical role in the development of the various seminars during the pilot phase, and suggestions were welcomed from the participants. Although the first two years of pilot programs tended to be quite structured and scheduled, much of the groundwork laid during these seminars was retained as permanent staff members joined NCCAT and assumed the continuing program development responsibilities (see Chapters 3-6).

Governance and Appropriations

The complicated issues of the governance and operation of the Center included not only where it would fit into the North Carolina higher education system, but the role of WCU and the development of facilities. The discussions of these ideas were an important part of many planning sessions and influenced both the Center's direction and leadership.

Throughout the entire planning period the future funding of the Center was a consideration for the members of the Planning Committee. Since the ARC funding was approved for only a designated period of planning and development time, it was imperative that legislative action establish placement of the Center at WCU and the funding at the budget level that would be required to maintain the Center as originally planned. In July 1985 the General Assembly approved $4.7 million for the proposed Center as part of $63.8 million for expansion of public schools in the biennial budget. Within the University of North Carolina budget was $500,000 in fiscal 1985-1986 and $2 million in 1986-1987 to cover operational expenses for the Center, including 35 staff positions. The public school portion of the allocation ($2.2 million), which did not begin until the second year of the budget, was to pay for substitute teachers, subsistence, and travel expenses for teachers participating in the Center's year-round programs. An additional $7.4 million was appropriated for construction (Denton, 1985).

At the request of Speaker Ramsey, members of the Planning Committee prepared the draft language for this special provision. A decision was made to identify the location of the Center at WCU in the legislation (North Carolina Center for the Advancement of Teaching, 1985), even though the president of the University of North Carolina, William Friday, wanted the UNC Board of Governors to have complete freedom concerning the organization and governance of the Center and the designation of a site. Some observers of this process claimed that the Center went to WCU because that was where Speaker Liston Ramsey wanted it placed, and his support was imperative in order to get other legislators to agree to the long-range funding needs of the Center. Ramsey's influence was recognized as extremely valuable and powerful as he worked with Hunt's office to make the Center a reality (H. F. Robinson, personal communication, February 18, 1988).

The only question that remained unanswered was whether the UNC Board of Governors would accept the appropriations and continue to support the Center. During a January 1985 meeting, a critical decision was made to defer consideration of whether to protest the inclusion of the Center in the Hunt budget on the grounds that the project had not been discussed with the Board of Governors. Although this sort of manipulation had happened before, as evidenced by the number of special projects the General Assembly had funded for other institutions, it was not the standard process in North Carolina (Board of Governors, 1985a). Fortunately for the development of the Center, the Board did not protest its inclusion in Hunt's budget, though this controversy would haunt the Center for many months. An editorial in the *News and Observer* read:

> Legislative budget-makers are threatening to erode a sound principle that undergirds the state university system. They do so by trying to circumvent the University of North Carolina Board of Governors and mandate that a new program for teachers be placed on a specific campus.

> The Joint Appropriations Expansion Budget Committee has approved spending $2.5 million over the next two years to establish a study center for elementary and secondary school teachers. Significantly, the committee has designated Western Carolina University in Cullowhee as the site for the facility. . . . The center also has powerful backers. Former Governor Hunt proposed it, recommended that WCU be the site and included it in his final budget package. House Speaker Liston Ramsey likes to attract such projects to his mountain district.
>
> And yet, the project has found its way into the proposed state budget without having gone through the UNC board's review process. This is no minor bureaucratic detail. Enacted by the 1971 General Assembly, the Higher Education Reorganization Act merged 16 separate institutions into the University of North Carolina and placed control in the Board of Governors. The board was established precisely to coordinate the university system rather than to have the campuses competing with each other like rival dukedoms.
>
> It is the job of the board and of the UNC administration to consider such questions as: Which campus is most suitable for a teachers' center? Could there be centers on more than one campus? What are the prospects for assembling a high quality staff to teach the teachers? It is not the job of lawmakers to set up projects on specific campuses by legislative fiat.
>
> By circumventing the Board of Governors, the legislature could create future problems as ideas for other projects arise. Let the merits of a teacher-study center be tested through the standard procedure, not handled as a mere piece of the legislative pork barrel.
>
> Of course, lawmakers have every right to scrutinize the UNC budget and to call on the university to help meet needs for which it is suited. Indeed, the legislature usually treats the university system generously. But the legislature ought to respect the principle under which the University of North Carolina system has operated with integrity. ("End Run," 1985, p. 28)

Ramsey explained that his thinking was "that the legislature has certain responsibilities. We are elected representatives of the people. How long do we wait? A hundred years? Still, nothing developed by this time, so the legislature had to act. Why wait if it's good? Why sit there and wait forever?" (personal communication, March 17, 1988).

Parties differed on how the Center should be affiliated with the University of North Carolina. Donald Stedman, representing UNC president William Friday, presented four models that could be considered for adoption. Stedman played a complicated role in the Center's planning because he reflected not only the senior staff of the University of North Carolina but also the Board of Governors. During the discussion on governance models, Stedman recommended a version that was finally adopted and that established a separate Board of Trustees for the Center: Eight members to be appointed by the Board of Governors of the University of North Carolina, two members each to be appointed by the lieutenant governor and the Speaker of the House of Representatives of the North Carolina General Assembly, and three *ex officio* members to include the president of the University of North Carolina, the chancellor of WCU, and the State Superintendent of Public Instruction (Board of Governors, 1985b).

A committee of the first Board of Trustees of the Center was charged with detailing the procedural and governance relationships between the Center's Board, the Board of Governors, and the Trustees of WCU. Some of the planners involved with NCCAT feared that the new governance regulations would prevent the Center from developing as they had envisioned. They believed that approval and authority might supersede the importance of the concept and purpose of the Center. Others maintained that it was the way that the University would show its control over NCCAT as a result of being left out of the appropriation process that had taken place many months earlier (M. McKinney, personal communication, March 24, 1988).

Evaluation and Decision Making

With planning for the first programs at the Center underway, William Cooley and William Bickel, senior scientists at the University of Pittsburgh's Learning Research and Development Center, were contracted by the Planning Committee to coordinate the evaluation component. After reviewing initial concept papers and partaking in discussions with the Planning Committee, Cooley and Bickel suggested questions for consideration in studying NCCAT's overall program. They encouraged the Planning Committee to define its primary client, to determine what services the Center would offer, and to set Center goals that were specific and manageable in number in an effort to assess the short- and long-range impact of the Center on its participants. Because of the Center's large budget, research on the retention of teachers in the classroom would be especially critical, and the cost effectiveness of various program models that were experimented with during the summer pilot programs would need to be examined (W. Bickel, personal communication, July 26, 1988).

Bickel outlined that the three major goals of the pilot and future seminars would be to assist teachers to acquire more positive attitudes toward teaching as their chosen profession, to feel more positively about themselves as persons, and to renew and sustain their interest in learning for learning's sake through the rediscovery of their ability to critically analyze intellectual issues.

Through the use of questionnaires and instruments adapted from the Purdue Teacher Opinionnaire (which assesses perceptions of teaching as a career), small-group discussions of participants' recommendations for program revisions, and observations of program sessions, Cooley and Bickel gathered information from the two sets of pilot programs that documented the overall impact of this type of program, reactions to specific features of the programs (e.g., extended weekend versus week-long, independent study versus structured program), and ways to improve the program (Cooley & Bickel, 1985).

At the conclusion of each set of pilot programs, an evaluation report was submitted to the planners. Bickel and Cooley underscored several themes that surfaced in reviewing the data on sessions and programs. A number of teachers were concerned about the intensity levels of the programming, the actual seminar setting and process, and the selection processes and criteria. The two evaluators placed particular emphasis on ways the Center could improve to meet its goals of retention, reward, and renewal. They found that informal written and oral comments overwhelmingly confirmed that the Center did indeed foster rejuvenation (see Chapter 6).

Recommendations for improving NCCAT were similar following both sets of pilot programs and included building more free time into the schedule, encouraging more discussion in both formal and informal groups, reducing the amount of reading material, and encouraging participant interaction early in the seminar. As previously identified by members of the Planning Committee, the evaluation confirmed the need for follow-up experiences for alumni. Other concrete recommendations provided by the evaluators were also recognized as important and were incorporated into the ongoing planning of programs by the Center's staff (Bickel, 1986; Bickel & Cooley, 1985; Cooley & Bickel, 1985).

Institutionalization: Planning in Perspective

With two summers of successful pilot programs completed, NCCAT staff implemented a year-round schedule of programs in the fall of 1986. A sound budget, permanent staff, governance plan, and facilities/building program were in place to enable the Center to move out of the "interim" stage. When the original budgets and plans for NCCAT were submitted, many people believed the funding and the scope of the project would be severely modified. Instead, the Center was funded at the full amount of the initial proposal, enabling it to become the only residential, state-funded program in the country for the renewal and reward of a state's best teachers. As project director and later interim director Gurney Chambers summed up this planning stage, "It turned out to be one of those things that happens only once in a lifetime, if that. Here's a dream, and the dream is fully realized" (personal communication, June 26, 1988).

In reflecting upon the creation of the Center, key elements come to mind. First and foremost, without the assertive leadership of Governor Hunt and the dedication of the members of the initial Planning Committee, it would most likely have remained a mere idea. Without the support and commitment of Liston Ramsey and other state legislators, the location and funding might have been compromised. Finally, the continued devotion of teachers who attended NCCAT speaks for itself. Many teachers claimed that NCCAT provided them with the "peak experience," a welcome change to the commonality of their work and conventional staff development (see Chapters 3, 4, and 6). With the national emphasis on educational reform, the time was right for a program that would break the traditional modes of teacher education by recognizing the importance of renewal. NCCAT was created to provide reward, intellectual stimulation, and teaching enhancement to excellent educators, with the belief that only when a teacher can feel the exhilaration of being valued and intellectually stimulated can he or she influence students in a like manner.

References

Appalachian Regional Commission (ARC). (1983, August). Findings from the conference on jobs and skills for the future, Washington, DC.

Appalachian Regional Commission (ARC). (1984). *A center for the advancement of teaching* (Contract # 84-113 NC-9178-84-81-302-08202). Unpublished contract, Office of the Governor of North Carolina.

Bickel, W. (1986, August). NCCAT: *Evaluation of summer 1986 programs*. Unpublished report, Learning Research and Development Center, University of Pittsburgh.

Bickel, W., & Cooley, W. (1985, October). *Evaluation of the center for the* advancement of teaching summer pilot programs: Supplemental report. Unpublished report, Learning Research and Development Center, University of Pittsburgh.

Board of Governors. (1985a, January 11). Unpublished minutes of meeting, Chapel Hill, North Carolina.

Board of Governors. (1985b, November 8). Unpublished minutes of meeting, Chapel Hill, North Carolina.

Cooley, W., & Bickel, W. (1985, August). *Preliminary report: Evaluation of the center for the advancement of teaching summer pilot programs*. Unpublished report, Learning Research and Development Center, University of Pittsburgh.

Denton, V. (1985, June 13). $4.7 million approved for teaching center at Western Carolina. *Asheville Citizen*, Section II, p. 13.

End run around UNC board. (1985, June 14). *News and Observer*, p. 28.

Hunt, J. (1984a, October 15). Executive order III: Planning committee for the center for the advancement of teaching. Office of the Governor, Raleigh, North Carolina.

Hunt, J. (1984b, December 11). Memo to the Commission on Education for Economic Growth. Unpublished, Office of the Governor, Raleigh, North Carolina.

Jackson, R. (1984, April 17). Letter to James Hunt. Unpublished, Office of the Governor, Raleigh, North Carolina.

Leland, E. (1984, November 13). Hunt proposes $16.8 billion 2-year budget. *News and Observer*, p. 1.

National Commission on Excellence in Education. (1983). *A nation at risk: The imperative for educational reform*. Washington, DC: U. S. Department of Education.

North Carolina Center for the Advancement of Teaching. (1985). N.C. Session Laws, 479-74.

North Carolina Commission on Education for Economic Growth (NCCEEG). (1984). *Education for economic growth: An action plan for North Carolina*. Raleigh: Author.

Owen, B. (1984a). *Excellence in education: The Hunt record 1977-83*. Office of the Governor, Raleigh, North Carolina.

Owen, B. (1984b, July). *A plan to develop a center for the advancement of teaching*. Unpublished proposal, Office of the Governor, Raleigh, North Carolina.

Owen, B. (1984c, November). *Center for the advancement of teaching*. Unpublished discussion paper, Office of the Governor, Raleigh, North Carolina.

Powell, J. P. (1983, November 29). Speech to the North Carolina Commission on Education for Economic Growth.

Report and Recommendations of the Planning Committee for the North Carolina Center for the Advancement of Teaching. (1985, September 11). Unpublished.

Stoltz, R., & McKinney, M. (1985a, April). *Summary of planning sessions on CAT programming*. Unpublished, Western Carolina University, Cullowhee.

Stoltz, R., & McKinney, M. (1985b, May). *Progress report*. Unpublished, Western Carolina University, Cullowhee.

Task Force on Education for Economic Growth. (1983). *Action for excellence: A comprehensive plan to improve our nation's schools*. Denver, CO: Education Commission of the States.

advancement of teaching summer pilot programs: Supplemental report. Unpublished report, Learning Research and Development Center, University of Pittsburgh.
Board of Governors. (1985a, January 11). Unpublished minutes of meeting, Chapel Hill, North Carolina.
Board of Governors. (1985b, November 8). Unpublished minutes of meeting, Chapel Hill, North Carolina.
Cooley, W., & Bickel, W. (1985, August). *Preliminary report: Evaluation of the center for the advancement of teaching summer pilot programs.* Unpublished report, Learning Research and Development Center, University of Pittsburgh.
Denton, V. (1985, June 13). $4.7 million approved for teaching center at Western Carolina. *Asheville Citizen*, Section II, p. 13.
End run around UNC board. (1985, June 14). *News and Observer*, p. 28.
Hunt, J. (1984a, October 15). Executive order III: Planning committee for the center for the advancement of teaching. Office of the Governor, Raleigh, North Carolina.
Hunt, J. (1984b, December 11). Memo to the Commission on Education for Economic Growth. Unpublished, Office of the Governor, Raleigh, North Carolina.
Jackson, R. (1984, April 17). Letter to James Hunt. Unpublished, Office of the Governor, Raleigh, North Carolina.
Leland, E. (1984, November 13). Hunt proposes $16.8 billion 2-year budget. *News and Observer*, p. 1.
National Commission on Excellence in Education. (1983). *A nation at risk: The imperative for educational reform.* Washington, DC: U. S. Department of Education.
North Carolina Center for the Advancement of Teaching. (1985). N.C. Session Laws, 479-74.
North Carolina Commission on Education for Economic Growth (NCCEEG). (1984). *Education for economic growth: An action plan for North Carolina.* Raleigh: Author.
Owen, B. (1984a). *Excellence in education: The Hunt record 1977-83.* Office of the Governor, Raleigh, North Carolina.
Owen, B. (1984b, July). *A plan to develop a center for the advancement of teaching.* Unpublished proposal, Office of the Governor, Raleigh, North Carolina.
Owen, B. (1984c, November). *Center for the advancement of teaching.* Unpublished discussion paper, Office of the Governor, Raleigh, North Carolina.
Powell, J. P. (1983, November 29). Speech to the North Carolina Commission on Education for Economic Growth.
Report and Recommendations of the Planning Committee for the North Carolina Center for the Advancement of Teaching. (1985, September 11). Unpublished.

Stoltz, R., & McKinney, M. (1985a, April). *Summary of planning sessions on CAT programming.* Unpublished, Western Carolina University, Cullowhee.

Stoltz, R., & McKinney, M. (1985b, May). *Progress report.* Unpublished, Western Carolina University, Cullowhee.

Task Force on Education for Economic Growth. (1983). *Action for excellence: A comprehensive plan to improve our nation's schools.* Denver, CO: Education Commission of the States.

Chapter 3

Building a Rationale for Teacher Renewal

ANTHONY G. RUD JR.

Today, public scrutiny has called attention to many of the problems of education, particularly in the public schools. However, it has not been without very serious side effects. Though the "second wave" of educational reform in the 1980s focused on the condition of the teacher, most of these reforms assumed deficiency rather than built on strength. The damage has been done. The incessantly critical "reformists" of the 1980s have contributed to the demoralization of teachers and other educators (see Sher, 1989).

Precollegiate teachers often have been seen as the transmitters of inert and approved knowledge (Darling-Hammond, 1985). This notion of the teacher as intellectual "gofer" has been particularly disheartening to committed veterans and capable prospective teachers alike. Drawing upon John Dewey (1916/1944), I propose the old idea that teachers should be seen primarily as learners and inquirers (Adler, 1990), and that education is fundamentally an activity of continuous renewal and exploration. An infectious enthusiasm nourished by cognitive and artistic adventures must be at the core of a teacher's world view.

One of the ways to nurture such enthusiasm is to provide support for periodic adventures of the mind at places like NCCAT and then to transform the local workplace through an emphasis on intellectual, artistic, and personal renewal in a collegial environment. As Lee Shulman states:

> All the talk of reforming schooling must never lose sight of the ultimate goal: to create institutions where students can learn through interaction with teachers who are themselves always learning. The effective school must become an educative setting for its teachers if it aspires to become an educational environment for its students. (1989, p. 186)

Central to my conception of teacher renewal is the idea of freedom. Initially considered from a cognitive angle, I shall expand and deepen this idea through consideration of the functions of artistic experience and of hospitality in educational settings. I shall then suggest briefly how teachers so renewed can interact effectively with educational reform.

A Rationale for Teacher Renewal

Knowledge for Freedom

First, let us pick up where Hoffbauer leaves off in her account of the early history of the Center (see Chapter 2). Shortly before full-time operation began, the newly hired residential faculty composed a rationale (Oldendorf, Rinnander, & Rud, 1986). Such an exercise did not lock us into a rigid code, but rather allowed for revision based on practice. Though the mandate establishing the Center spoke of advanced study in the liberal arts, it did not commit us to a fully articulated philosophical base. Thus, as pioneer faculty, we were granted uncommon freedom in composing this rationale.

We stated that the broadest purpose of the Center was to increase freedom for teachers through knowledge gained in study and informed discourse. By freedom we had in mind the internal, cognitive freedom Dewey termed "freedom of intelligence" (1938/1963, p. 61). We noted that recent trends in teacher training and certification have steadily decreased the amount of freedom of intelligence enjoyed by teachers (Shulman, 1986). Behavioral training programs and curricular objectives can produce predictable outcomes, but they diminish what could be the robust range of teaching, where minds are active and encouraged to seek out the edges of knowledge. Teaching implies mastery not only of performance and procedure, but also of content and rationale; the teacher should employ reasoned judgment rather than just display prescribed behavior. Overwhelming demands on the time and energies of our teachers too often inhibit intellectual growth and renewal (Shulman, 1989; Sizer, 1984). Our vision is that efforts toward teacher renewal can help to reverse these trends.

We initially saw the type of teacher we wanted to encourage exemplified in what Lee Shulman (1986) and his colleagues were trying to accomplish at Stanford in their "wisdom of practice" studies. Shulman's team set out to describe the particular type of knowledge shown by expert teachers, which they call "pedagogical content knowledge" (Shulman, 1986, pp. 9-10). This is the type of expertise exhibited by teachers "wise in practice" when teaching *Moby Dick* to a particular group of students; those teachers will adjust their presentations and discussions to the needs of the students. Shulman's team saw that this is the crucial knowledge of a teacher, beyond the first level of knowledge of subject matter. Shulman's work, then, shifts the focus of research on teaching to ideas ("teacher thinking") and away from behaviors. Teaching is recognized once more as an enterprise of the mind.

At NCCAT we believed that we were working with people adept at such teaching. Our participants are exemplary teachers, self-selected and then screened via a rigorous application, who have worked full-time in the classroom for at least 3 years. We did not presume that we could improve or enhance their pedagogy. They had come to us as competent and even outstanding teachers.

That we work with such teachers may admittedly be a limitation to our discussion. However, we did notice that an "overarching" quality of intellect and attitude is decisive for our work and for the free individuals that we are attempting to allow our teachers to be. We wanted to foster curiosity in learning, a recognition of ambiguity, a taste for finding and creating meaning in the world, and a relish for sharing that meaning with others in conversation, writing, or art. Our work at NCCAT has been guided by the unstated maxim that a passionate intellect is a necessary condition for excellent teaching. Like Spinoza's substance, this intellectual "substance" provides the heart for any further attributes, talents, or wise practices.

Peak Learning Experiences

There was one seeming obstacle to our work. We realized that we had only a short period of time to engage our participants. Typically they would be at the Center for 4 or 5 days. The life of the mind is subtle; how could zestful learning be enhanced or revived in so short a time? We were all more than a bit skeptical that we could accomplish this goal. However, the extent and depth of the reactions of our participants to the learning experience have been surprising. Data given to our outside evaluators (see Chapter 6) indicate that often time spent at the Center was pivotal in determining the course and intensity of a teacher's subsequent intellectual and professional development.

What Benjamin Bloom (1981) has described as a "peak learning experience," a powerful and memorable "moment of truth" that can affect the course of one's life and education, may have indeed occurred for a number of teacher participants at the Center. These experiences are characterized by cognitive concentration and emotional intensity. They may even be revelatory of a life's work. Many of our participants report such experiences, particularly in regard to their desire to continue as teachers.

Initial Precepts for Practice

The initial rationale took into account the importance of a Deweyan freedom of intelligence and the possibility of peak learning experiences. We stated five precepts to guide our work. In the following sections, I shall examine these precepts in light of more than 4 years of practice. This will allow the reader to see how the rationale has been developed.

To be effective in enhancing a teacher's intellectual growth within the time constraints of the seminars, we stipulated and stressed certain critical precepts about the nature of teaching and learning. These interrelated precepts concern the nature of knowledge, interdisciplinary teaching and learning, norms of reflective and critical thinking, a community of inquiry, and the teacher as learner and inquirer.

The Nature of Knowledge

Each seminar should examine and explore the nature of knowledge as it is understood in the modern sciences, humanities, and the arts. Through the seminars teachers are encouraged to recognize that every field has within itself divergent viewpoints on what constitutes knowledge, and that education itself is no exception to this generalization. In exploring multiple paths of knowledge, participants also develop skills of analytical thinking by distinguishing among various points of view. Our programs should seek to assemble participants representing multiple points of view, thereby encouraging the need for integration and synthesis. Within a single field, such as physics, there are differing points of view and competing theories. Exploration of why a particular point of view is dominant in a field and of the competing claims of other views allows one to see that multiple perspectives are possible.

For example, the field of moral education was until recently an area of curricular interest dominated by discussion of moral stages and "values clarification." These theories and practices themselves had supplanted to a great degree other competing claims, most notably traditional religious moral education. Two more competing models have emerged recently: character education (Ryan & Greer, 1989) and a perspective that emphasizes narrative and the "different voice" of female development (Gilligan, 1982; Noddings, 1984; Tappan & Brown, 1989).

Interdisciplinary Teaching and Learning

The Center should present topics of an interdisciplinary nature, unlikely to be available in textbooks or confined to a single academic field. In this way participants are encouraged to interpret information from multiple perspectives using a variety of paradigms. A similar method is used in seminars in which a familiar topic is examined using new methodologies or in light of new questions. The basic change in history, from asking "What happened in the French Revolution?" to asking "What happened to which people in the French Revolution?" is an example of how a seminar might be focused to show that the type of questions asked can actually shape the nature of the discipline.

Material of this nature should be taught in an interactive manner. When one is presented with several perspectives (historical, scientific, literary) on a topic (the culture of India), there is potential for comparisons and syntheses among the various perspectives. This potential can be exploited by a discussion leader sensitive to a multifaceted topic. Such teaching does not result in pellets of easily digestible information or even foundational truth. Rather, an "edifying" conversation has a chance to occur (Arcilla, 1990; Rorty, 1989, 1990). Such openness can lead to the entertainment of possibilities, as discussed in the first precept.

Norms of Reflective and Critical Thinking

The Center is primarily concerned with the development of adequate and comprehensive means to understand the world, and in accord with that concern it attempts to ensure that seminars include opportunities for reflective, critical thinking. That is not to say that one does not learn facts or generalizations while developing new intellectual structures. The delight in learning, where the whole world opens up as an object for contemplation and mastery, is part of intellectual development, as new structures crave new phenomena (Buchmann, 1989, 1990; Duckworth, 1987).

Such delight in learning demands a wide epistemological net. Many teachers come to the Center accustomed to what might be called a "pre-philosophical" or "pre-reflective" stance toward the world. This stance is partly characterized by the following:

1. Science describes the world as it really is.
2. Its pursuit is a theory- and value-free incremental task of slowly but surely filling in the details of the world "out there."
3. Ideas concerning what to value are matters of personal concern.
4. Appeal to authority in such matters is an often-taken avenue.

Through the type of discussion described in the first and second precepts, participants can come to the point where they can loosen their grip on these and other tenets and realize that there are many paths to knowledge. There are deep disagreements in all fields, born of the vitality of inquiry. By becoming a student again, one can enlarge the capacity to both learn areas foreign to one's background and expertise, and enter into a supportive and trusting community devoted to learning (Palmer, 1983).

Our "Taxonomy of NCCAT Thinking Skills and Dispositions" was developed to guide such discussions.

- listening for the structure of an argument
- giving others time to respond
- respecting silence
- challenging what the person says, not the person
- "piggybacking"; building upon what another person says
- recognizing what is essential or paradigmatic in discrete or particular facts or anecdotes
- evaluating claims based upon their merit and not their source (particularly apropos of "visiting experts" or other claims to authority)
- evaluating claims based upon their merit and not their emotional intensity
- asking for clarification of assertions made by presenters
- analyzing the components of a presentation
- comparing divergent presentations or discussions
- synthesizing the components of a seminar, while also respecting divergent viewpoints
- striving to articulate the theme or "steel rod" of a seminar session or entire seminar
- dwelling with ambiguity and tension as aspects of a complex mind

The Community of Inquiry

By bringing together heterogeneous groups of 20 teachers, we are able to form what Matthew Lipman (Lipman, Sharp, & Oscanyan,

1980) calls a "community of inquiry." With the proper cues from staff and presenters, our participants are able to learn from each other, while developing the crucial skill of listening to an opposing viewpoint, formulating a response, and defending that response by marshalling evidence in a well-formed argument. This takes practice, but if encouraged by a facilitator, participants can begin to realize something precious and rare in the life of the mind: the elation that comes from the discussion of opposing viewpoints in an atmosphere of attention, trust, curiosity, and fellow-feeling.

We are well situated in the southern Appalachian mountains to be able to try to accomplish these ends. The mountaintop is a common metaphor in religious and philosophical literature for a disengagement from and reflection upon everyday life, and many teachers see the Center's location in just this fashion.

Seminars often close with a session devoted to the implications of the discussion for the lives of the participants. Networks of seminar alumni have been established to further communication and to encourage mutual support in the life of the mind. Periodic reunions are arranged to renew and support the work of the initial seminar, and encouragement should be provided for school-based programs that would augment and perhaps even replace traditional staff development (see Chapter 4). An example could be the kind of learning group called a "study circle" that in Sweden provides adults with a program of voluntary, government-supported reading groups.

The Teacher as Learner and Inquirer

The resident faculty of Center fellows and the visiting presenters should exemplify what is new and zestful in their teaching. The fellows should serve as models for the participants by trying out new ideas and new pedagogies (Sykes, 1988). Engagement in wide-ranging research, writing, artistic production, and a sharing and appreciation of each other's work are excellent preparation for outstanding teaching. The fellows, who are actively engaged in learning, can share with participants the fruits of their reading and artistry and how this shapes their own teaching and learning.

Our seminars allow participants to take intellectual and personal risks as they explore areas that may be foreign to them. We do not provide instruction in pedagogy; rather, in modeling the best in seminar teaching and collegial leadership, we make it possible for participants to take away our own "hidden curriculum."

We encourage seminar participants to devise their own learning projects, to become active in professional associations, and to view the creation of knowledge and the enhancement of artistic production as an ongoing process. As a presenter in an early program declared, the most eminent scientists retain the curious questioning attitude of a 10-year-old child. Let such thinkers, at once learned and eager for more knowledge, be the models for our teachers and students.

Thus the Center symbolizes the link between the world of the university and the world of precollegiate education. The Center fellows are hybrids formed from these two spheres of education. However, the faculty at NCCAT have several advantages. Our programs do not compete with the university, as we offer no grades or credits. Participants initially deferential to Center faculty realized that we had no power over them (Rinnander, 1988). With the falling away of the traditional trappings of higher education, we too have felt liberated. We strive for conversation, which ideally is the essence of university education but rarely occurs in that context (Wilshire, 1990).

The Rationale in Practice

Several years ago we offered a seminar entitled "A Geologist's View of Water Resources." It was led by a university geologist, who conducted discussions and several field experiences. Many of the participants had selected this seminar as one of their backup choices, and they had come somewhat reluctantly. They wondered out loud whether a week spent on the topic of water would be fun or even interesting. As they saw just how complex and vital water resources are and how water pervades not only our daily life but also our art, they began to really delve into the material. Several days were spent out in the field examining a dying mountain lake and measuring stream velocity with homemade instruments. Time was given over to discussing water in works of art and to a demonstration and discussion of controversial "water divining." The phenomenon of water in its many manifestations was encountered directly. Several of those novice hydrologists have since told us how science never seemed so new and exciting to them.

Knee deep in a mountain stream, participants could experience the type of teaching and learning advocated by Eleanor Duckworth in her essay "Teaching as Research."

> So what is the role of teaching if knowledge must be constructed by each individual? In my view, there are two aspects to teaching. The first is to put students into contact with phenomena related to the

area to be studied—the real thing, not books or lectures about it—
and to help them notice what is interesting; to engage them so they
will continue to think and wonder about it. The second is to have the
students try to explain the sense they are making, and instead of
explaining things to students, to try to understand their sense. These
two aspects are, of course, interdependent: When people are engaged in the matter, they try to explain it and in order to explain it
they seek out more phenomena that will shed light on it. (1987,
p. 123)

The original phenomena, whether they are discovered in a literary
work or a cold mountain stream, invite the construction of an interpretation. The more dissonant the phenomena, the more opportunity
exists to challenge existing frames of reference. For example, in
another seminar, a discussion of artificial intelligence guided by the
theme "computers and the human spirit" (Turkle, 1984) was prefaced
by consecutive visits to an automated truck axle factory and the home
of poet Carl Sandburg. The two ways of knowing—the abstract world
of the computer programmer and the robot and the concrete world of
the poet—were not compared until later, thereby allowing teachers to
construct their own interpretations and evaluations of the phenomena.

The Construction of Reflective Self-Knowledge

Extracting knowledge from the "real thing" and the communication of that knowledge referred to by Duckworth can also be a process
that is turned reflectively upon oneself. Such a process is an ideal result
of the themes of the rationale so far stated. This further stage of
teacher development can be a kind of teaching that is renewing in
itself.

Perhaps the most thoroughly developed example of such reflective knowledge derived from teaching is Vivian Gussin Paley. Paley's
practice is the ideal of the reflective teacher who is constantly bent
upon the improvement not only of practice through such reflection,
but also is devoted to the sharpening and deepening of her own
intellect, and the sharing of that intellect with others.

Paley (1986), a veteran elementary school teacher and recipient of
a MacArthur award, describes candidly her lack of interest and enjoyment in her early years of teaching. She happened to observe a colleague using the "old Socratic method" (p. 123) she too had once used
as a Great Books discussion leader. Paley then began to realize how
excited she was about the process of thinking going on in the minds of

her students. She now affirms the place of this process over any outcome, or product, in her teaching (personal communication, January 20, 1990).

The impetus for her renewed interest and curiosity about her own teaching came from the hard realization that she did not know the answers to the questions that her young students were posing. Paley was thus forced to keep asking relevant questions, based not on her own preconceptions, but rather on how the child was thinking about a topic (personal communication, January 20, 1990; 1986, p. 124).

Yet Paley the teacher goes beyond a Socratic pose in the classroom. She turns the questioning back upon herself and her own thinking with a "specific tool," the tape recorder. Paley tapes 90 minutes of her students' stories and the accompanying dialogue each day. In transcribing the taped dialogue, large chunks of which appear in her books, she has the opportunity to review all that went on in the classroom. Using what she calls an "internalized Socratic method" (Obermiller, 1989, p. 19), Paley takes herself to task in preparation for her writing (personal communication, January 20, 1990). This exhausting teaching, taping, and transcribing regimen is an important living manifestation of the Socratic notion of the examined life, of reflective inquiry aimed at self-knowledge.

Art and Hospitality in Teacher Renewal

Though such reflective self-knowledge may be a culmination of the initial precepts, evolution of this rationale has continued in the early years of our work with teachers. The largely cognitive and discipline-oriented components of the early rationale have been augmented with additional emphasis on the personal and emotional needs of veteran, exemplary teachers. Turning to what Bruner (1962) has called the "left hand" of intuition and art, I shall concentrate on two paths in the development of the rationale: (1) the role of artistic experience and aesthetic contemplation, and (2) the importance of a pervasive ethos of hospitality. I show how the dialectic of thought, art, and hospitality can be related to the idea of freedom in the initial rationale.

As discussed above and in Chapter 1, much of the early theoretical work at the Center focused on determining the role of reflective, critical thinking. Though aesthetic experience was an early theme of our work (McPherson, Rinnander, & Rud, 1987, p. 48), it soon became central and pronounced. As our seminar offerings widened, we included not only text-driven "great books" seminars and experiential scientific activities, but also programs that had core elements of artistic production and aesthetic contemplation.

Early seminars on dance and myth challenged the heavily cognitive orientation of the rationale. These programs often culminated in an artistic product, such as a set of totemic masks. Participants spent a week with an internationally known choreographer and members of the American Dance Festival. They created a dance to be performed and recorded at the end of their stay. Though there was some discussion of the dance, reflective conversation around a seminar table was not a prominent part of this program.

What did emerge was the recognition that artistic production can be just as valuable for renewal as reflective, critical discussion. However, such a recognition seemed to conflict with an underlying assumption of the rationale concerning the creation of a community of inquiry based on shared discourse. We thought that this community, composed of individuals with divergent backgrounds and abilities, should be cemented by the bond of common discourse.

Social cohesion forged through common discourse and perhaps even the seeking of a common good may leave little room for individual enrichment and the celebration of the idiosyncratic. These are the hallmarks of the sort of freedom found in aesthetic experience and artistic production. In an account used successfully in several seminars, Goethe described the ecstasy found on his journey to Italy (1962/1830). His break from the routine of a civil servant, and the fostering of the freedom of the imagination during that trip into light and sun, is a forceful reminder of the renewing power of art.

The emphasis on art extended the original rationale and forced some of us to reflect upon its powerful role. We underscore with Dewey the importance of freedom of intelligence. Yet art is the free work of the imagination that often, though not always, results in a private and idiosyncratic experience. It involves a sort of freedom hinted at by Kant and more fully explored by thinkers such as Schiller (Gardiner, 1979). Our community of inquiry improves upon the cognition of the individual, while in art the experience is highly personal and often private. Art, therefore, can be seen as complementary to the shared experiences that arise out of discourse.

I began by discussing the intellectual aspects of a renewal program for teachers. Art grants us occasion to move away from the discussion table, to go out into the surroundings, and to transform these surroundings by creating works of art. Such material and artistic aspects of the surroundings—a flower arrangement, a poem, a quartet of teachers playing chamber music—can be tokens for comfort and trust in a learning environment (see Chapter 1). In the following section, I develop what I call "learning in comfort," or hospitality in an educational setting. Hospitality has important ethical and epistemological aspects that relate material aspects of comfort to cognitive and artistic aspects of the rationale already discussed.

Learning in Comfort: Developing an Ethos of Hospitality

The word "hospitality" conjures up several associations. We may think of the literary conventions of hospitality so important in medieval French romances, or perhaps our present-day "hospitality industry," or, as Henri Nouwen says, a "soft sweet kindness, tea parties, bland conversation, and a general atmosphere of coziness" (1975, p. 47). I am talking about something different. Learning in comfort and trust is a crucial aspect of teacher renewal and, as Griffin points out, a neglected facet of our schools (see Chapter 7).

The combination of learning and hospitality comes in part from the tradition of the Benedictine monastery (Rinnander, 1988, p. 54). Our conscious use of the term *hospitality* in our work at the Center, however, has only recently been made an explicit part of our theory. The practice of being a host is connected to our initial rationale and to the importance of art through its relationship to freedom.

Our programs are marked by careful attention to the comfort and security of our participants. Even in our outdoor excursions (see the narrative in Chapter 4), comfort in a new and potentially uncomfortable setting is taken into account. Here, just as around the seminar table, it is more important to have the opportunity to try something new in a supportive environment than to be unduly challenged and confronted by nature.

Henri Nouwen speaks about hospitality in a learning context.

> Hospitality . . . means primarily the creation of a free space where the stranger can enter and become a friend instead of an enemy. Hospitality is not to change people, but to offer them space where change can take place. . . .
>
> Teaching, therefore, asks first of all the creation of a space where students and teachers can enter into a fearless communication with each other and allow their respective life experiences to be their primary and most valuable source of growth and maturation. . . .
>
> The hospitable teacher has to reveal to students that they have something to offer. . . . A good host is the one who believes that his

guest is carrying a promise he wants to reveal to anyone who shows genuine interest. (1975, pp. 51, 60, 61)

Nouwen stresses the connotations of the Dutch word for hospitality, translated as "freedom of the guest." This is exactly the sense of the word I would like to emphasize for its import for education. If we are concerned with the material support for a free and "fearless communication," how should we go about it in schools and elsewhere?

Let us look more closely at the Center's means of achieving this end. We attend to the comfort and security of our participants with small "tokens of respect," such as a name on the door, a newspaper, and a small basket of fruit to greet them. The organization of a program complements these tokens. Once the seminar begins, format and content are open for discussion. Participants can suggest changes in the seminar format in the "Response to the Day" segment. A number of seminars have been reorganized to account for the need for more extended discussion or free time (see the narrative in Chapter 4). For teachers used to a crowded schedule, this is often the first time they have been entrusted with free time to use solely for their own benefit (McPherson, Rinnander, & Rud, 1987).

Edward Milner's poem in Chapter 5 evokes the vulnerability revealed by teachers who, in visiting a place for their own renewal, recognize it as a home for learning. I shall end this section with similar words from another participant/guest, Dixie Dellinger, a high school English teacher, in a letter to me.

> To me, the Center represents a marvelous phenomenon in which the concrete mirrors the abstract and makes it visible. One's physical needs are taken care of—wonderful meals and tranquil, comfortable surroundings—and one's intellectual needs recognized and also wonderfully fed. In that respect, it becomes a metaphor—a "center" in the truest sense in which we as teachers can reach our own "centers."
>
> But a thing most admirable in the concept of the Center is its trust in teachers, something that is becoming ever more rare in the institution of public education. The Center assumes that teachers are intellectually inclined, that they are thinkers, that they are capable and honorable, and it demonstrates these assumptions in its programming and its arrangements. (personal communication, August 1987)

Art, Cognition, and Hospitality in Practice

As artistic experience and hospitality have become important themes that have deepened our work, they have entered into a dialectic with cognition, unified by the idea of freedom.

Teacher: I want to put a Japanese maple over there next to the building.
Landscape Architect: Hold on a minute. Are you sure that you want that kind of tree there?
Teacher: Well, I really like the way it looks, so full, and when the leaves turn red . . .
Landscape Architect: Wait, let's go back to your plan and consider these elements: Where is the sun going to be and what else is around that part of the plan? You have got the start of a good scheme for the area, but I want you to consider the total picture . . .
Second Teacher: We did consider exposure to the sun . . . here, look at our plan. The trellis helps to control the sun, see, and we are going to work with evergreen shrubs over there . . .

"The Design of Earthly Gardens," a seminar held in the spring of 1990, dealt with landscape architecture. Activities included discussion of the history of the term itself, beginning with its use by Frederick Law Olmstead in the late nineteenth century and ending with discussion of the merits of new forms of landscaping. We stressed that landscaping was not a static field, but was reflective of society and the world at a particular time. The magnificent gardens of Biltmore Estate in Asheville, North Carolina, reflect both the man who commissioned them (George Vanderbilt) and the man who designed them (Frederick Law Olmstead).

The core activity of the week, however, was not discussion but rather the design of the common area between the new NCCAT residence halls, which were still under construction at that time. Led by a team of landscape architects, small groups of teachers analyzed the site and drew up plans for its improvement through landscape elements. This area, fresh from completion by construction workers, invited participants to think of ways to make a stark, uninviting space of concrete and steel a place where future participants could meet and share social occasions.

Factors such as exposure to the sun and flow of traffic had to be figured into the plan, as did the special characteristics of the living plants that could be used to enhance the area. The dialectic of thought, art, and hospitality manifested itself in the plans of the teachers for the site. Each plan was discussed and analyzed when presented to the full group. Elements from each plan will be incorporated into the final design for the space, to serve as a token of hospitality writ large.

Reform, Renewal, and Educational Leadership

Before closing, let us turn to a sketch of a view of educational leadership, to be extended and deepened in Chapter 5, that is linked to the rationale examined in this chapter. I briefly examine recent theories of administration that may help to aid such an effort in the schools themselves.

A core theme of this book concerns the possible relationship of such renewal activities within the broad currents of educational reform. Though we have stressed the fundamental difference between the two activities (see Chapter 1), underlying this distinction is the starting place for linkage. Renewal activities that allow the teacher the freedom of learning and inquiry must precede or at least work in tandem with the efforts of educational reform. Why is this the case?

Phillip Schlechty has given an apt description of how reform and renewal interact. In a visit, he described the experiential liberal arts programs at NCCAT as "studied indifference" to the work of educational reform.

A closer examination of his own work can reveal what he means. The staff development unit he formerly directed, the Gheens Professional Development Academy in Louisville, Kentucky (Schlechty, Ingwerson, & Brooks, 1988), provides technical assistance to schools and develops leadership in order to move toward the goal of transforming the local workplace into an area of vitality and hoped-for success for all students. Teachers are seen as leaders, and teaching itself is renewing much in the way it is for Vivian Paley. The teachers enable the students to learn to be the workers on the material (curriculum). Schlechty believes that in tandem with such work, there should be opportunities for teachers to freely expand their intellectual horizons and to take both personal and intellectual risks in an atmosphere of trust and support.

This is precisely how renewal must undergird reform. For teachers to believe they have a stake in the improvement of an institution, they must see that the institution has a stake in, or cares about, them as people and as intelligent, capable human beings. This reciprocal relationship of caring is based on the belief that if you give unconditionally to an individual or teacher, as a mother does to her child, that person will be more likely to give back (Noddings, 1984). This reciprocity of care enhances both the institution (school) and the teachers (McPherson, 1988).

Given the way schools are organized, this reciprocal relationship can best be initiated through the administration of schools. Yet there still exists an enormous gulf between teachers and their administrators in our public schools. The causes of this gap are certainly varied and complex. Increased burdens placed upon the public schools, from governmental regulation to societal expectations, often have made teaching onerous and the administration of schools joyless.

What may be necessary is a reorganized model of school administration. Recent theoretical research in the area of educational administration (McPherson, 1988; Sergiovanni, 1989) points to the type of leadership complementary to the model of the teacher advocated in this chapter. Educational leadership must go beyond what Sergiovanni refers to as "bartering," where teachers and administrators exchange actions and services as if they were currency. Such leadership, he argues, produces only predictable and mediocre results (1989, pp. 215-216).

Furthermore, taking into account the argument of this chapter, such leadership would not take advantage of the autonomous, zestful learners and creators promoted through a program of teacher renewal. Sergiovanni, following James MacGregor Burns, advocates "transformative" leadership (1989, pp. 214-217). This kind of leadership emphasizes expectations of what one can become and a shared covenant based on moral commitment that will lead toward excellence in schooling.

Sergiovanni's vision of administrators and teachers bonded by covenant and directed to extraordinary and shared achievement is a powerful image. Whether it can be achieved in the schools is another matter. I suggest that zestful learners, uniting in fearless discourse, learning in comfort, and being graced through art, might be good candidates to begin to enact this vision. Those learners can, and should, be our teachers.

References

Adler, M. (1990). Beyond indoctrination: The quest for genuine learning. In D. Dill and Associates, *What teachers need to know: The knowledge, skills, and values essential to good teaching* (pp. 157-165). San Francisco: Jossey-Bass.

Arcilla, R. (1990). Edification, conversation, and narrative: Rortyan motifs for philosophy of education. *Educational Theory, 40*(1), 35-39.

Bloom, B. (1981). Peak learning experiences. In *All our children learning* (pp. 193-199). New York: McGraw-Hill.

Bruner, J. (1962). *On knowing: Essays for the left hand.* Cambridge, MA: Harvard University Press.

Buchmann, M. (1989). The careful vision: How practical is contemplation in teaching? *American Journal of Education, 98*(1), 35-61.

Buchmann, M. (1990). Beyond the lonely, choosing will: Professional development in teacher thinking. *Teachers College Record, 91*(4), 481-508.

Darling-Hammond, L. (1985). Valuing teachers: The making of a profession. *Teachers College Record, 87*(2), 205-218.

Dewey, J. (1944). *Democracy and education.* New York: Macmillan. (Original work published 1916)

Dewey, J. (1963). *Experience and education.* New York: Macmillan. (Original work published 1938)

Duckworth, E. (1987). Teaching as research. In *"The having of wonderful ideas" and other essays on teaching and learning* (pp. 122-140). New York: Teachers College Press.

Gardiner, P. (1979). Freedom as an aesthetic idea. In A. Ryan (Ed.), *The idea of freedom* (pp. 27-39). Oxford: Oxford University Press.

Gilligan, C. (1982). *In a different voice: Psychological theory and women's development.* Cambridge, MA: Harvard University Press.

Goethe, J. (1962). *Italian journey, 1786-88.* (W. H. Auden & E. Mayer, Trans.). New York: Pantheon. (Original work published 1830)

Lipman, M., Sharp, A. M., & Oscanyan, F. S. (1980). *Philosophy in the classroom.* Philadelphia: Temple University Press.

McPherson, R. B. (1988). The superintendent and the problem of delegation. *Peabody Journal of Education, 65*(4), 113-130.

McPherson, R. B., Rinnander, J., & Rud, A. (1987). To the heart of the mind: Renewal for North Carolina teachers. *Educational Leadership, 45*(3), 43-48.

Noddings, N. (1984). *Caring: A feminine approach to ethics and moral education.* Berkeley: University of California Press.

Nouwen, H. (1975). *Reaching out: The three movements of the spiritual life.* Garden City, NY: Doubleday.

Obermiller, T. (1989, Summer). All in a day's play. *University of Chicago Magazine, 81*(4), 15-19.

Oldendorf, W., Rinnander, J., & Rud, A. (1986). NCCAT seminars for teachers: Knowledge for freedom: A preliminary rationale by the NCCAT fellows. Cullowhee, NC: NCCAT.

Paley, V. (1986). On listening to what the children say. *Harvard Educational Review, 56*(2), 122-131.

Palmer, P. (1983). *To know as we are known: A spirituality of education.* San Francisco: Harper & Row.

Rinnander, J. (1988). Vision and person in teacher renewal. *Proceedings of the South Atlantic Philosophy of Education Society*, pp. 50-56.

Rorty, R. (1989). *Contingency, irony, and solidarity*. Cambridge: Cambridge University Press.

Rorty, R. (1990). The dangers of over-philosophication: Reply to Arcilla and Nicholson. *Educational Theory, 40*(1), 41-44.

Ryan, K., & Greer, P. (1989). Something is not out there. *Action in Teacher Education, 11*(1), 11-15.

Schlechty, P., Ingwerson, D., & Brooks, T. (1988). Inventing professional development schools. *Educational Leadership, 46*(3), 28-31.

Sergiovanni, T. (1989). The leadership needed for quality schooling. In T. Sergiovanni & J. Moore (Eds.), *Schooling for tomorrow: Directing reforms to issues that count* (pp. 213-226). Boston: Allyn & Bacon.

Sher, J. (1989, February 22). Blue ribbon panels lack "moral authority." *Education Week*, pp. 25, 36.

Shulman, L. (1986). Those who understand: Knowledge growth in teaching. *Educational Researcher, 15*(2), 4-14.

Shulman, L. (1989). Teaching alone, learning together: Needed agendas for the new reforms. In T. Sergiovanni & J. Moore (Eds.), *Schooling for tomorrow: Directing reforms to issues that count* (pp. 166-187). Boston: Allyn & Bacon.

Sizer, T. (1984). *Horace's compromise: The dilemma of the American high school*. Boston: Houghton Mifflin.

Sykes, G. (1988). Inspired teaching: The missing element in "effective schools." *Educational Administration Quarterly, 24*(4), 461-469.

Tappan, M., & Brown, L. (1989). Stories told and lessons learned: Toward a narrative theory of moral development and moral education. *Harvard Educational Review, 59*(2), 182-205.

Turkle, S. (1984). *The second self: Computers and the human spirit*. New York: Simon & Schuster.

Wilshire, B. (1990). *The moral collapse of the university: Professionalism, purity, and alienation*. Albany: State University of New York Press.

Chapter 4

Adventures for the Intellect

WALTER P. OLDENDORF

The several hundred adventures for the intellect created at the North Carolina Center for the Advancement of Teaching since 1985 have ranged across a broad spectrum of the arts, sciences, and humanities, reflecting the diverse backgrounds and interests of the Center faculty, the dynamic philosophical base of the Center, the breadth of the original mandate, and the evaluative input of the program alumni. One of the most significant and interesting aspects of this curriculum lies in its contrast to more traditional models of educational reform. The NCCAT curriculum differs in fundamental ways from mainstream American metaphors of the nature of teaching and learning, and one thrust of this chapter will be to underscore and illustrate those differences.

The first section will examine the metaphor of cultural transmission that underlies most current thinking about educational reform in America and will show the principal ways in which the NCCAT curriculum model rests on different metaphors—those of progressivism, disciplinary initiation, and vocation. NCCAT has developed its programs on the central premise that learning is rewarding on its own, freed from formal requirements, exams, grades, and credits, and that premise has proven to be viable. Most important, NCCAT is distinguished from reform programs in its assumption that rather than repair, reeducation, or rehabilitation, teachers need opportunities to develop their unfulfilled potentials as talented, creative individuals. The disciplinary initiation model of curriculum developed by Prakash and Waks (1985), and the progressivist model of Kohlberg and Mayer (1972) are helpful in understanding how the NCCAT curriculum contrasts with the transmissionist metaphor of education. This section closes with quotes from Dwayne Huebner's (1987) essay, which asserts that understanding how we can improve teaching as a vocation requires far more than the usual notions of more and better knowledge, methods, materials, and organization.

In the second section of this chapter I give a detailed description of a recent NCCAT seminar, "Humans on Earth: The Blue Ridge Experience." I tell the story of the seminar as a way of illustrating the qualitative aspects of our programs as well as demonstrating the ways in which our undergirding principles are implemented in practice.

In conclusion I take a broader look at the NCCAT curriculum, giving examples of the variety of topics as well as the various types of programs. I discuss briefly the newest Center program, global alumni seminars.

Center Curriculum

The conceptual frameworks for considering models of curriculum developed by Kohlberg and Mayer (1972) and by Prakash and Waks (1985) provide an effective scheme for analyzing the Center's curriculum. I argue that the Center's program is not sharply delineated by any one model, but that aspects of what Kohlberg and Mayer call progressivism, and what Prakash and Waks term disciplinary initiation, are clearly present. I want to emphasize those aspects because they distinguish NCCAT from the mainstream of educational reform.

Kohlberg and Mayer's analysis is self-consciously rooted in the tradition begun by John Dewey (1956/1902), when he described the contrasting notions of a subject matter curriculum and a child-centered curriculum. Dewey then went on to suggest a more adequate approach that would recognize the interactive nature of both child and subject matter in constructing the curriculum (pp. 4-14). Kohlberg and Mayer extend this analysis to provide a taxonomy of major figures in the history of twentieth-century education.

The subject matter tradition, termed cultural transmissionism by Kohlberg and Mayer, rests on the metaphor of the human as *tabula rasa*, the blank slate upon which the teacher writes. More recently, the metaphor has taken the shape of the human as an information processing machine, more or less complicated, which receives knowledge from the environment or teachers. Knowledge consists of the facts, principles, and generalizations about the external, observable world that are primarily based in sense data. The job of the teacher is to transmit knowledge in the most effective and efficient manner, and the role of the learner is to be a passive recipient of that knowledge.

The cultural transmissionist metaphor continues as the technical model of the school in the work of Prakash and Waks (1985). The technical model of the school described by Prakash and Waks is the "image of education as rational production, as the efficient adjustment of productive means to determinate measurable ends" (pp. 81-82).

They list the all too familiar characteristics of school reform mandates of the 1980s: emphasis on memory and problem-solving routines. Knowledge becomes the acquisition of facts, and understanding the ability to apply cognitive routines. Excellence is defined in terms of student achievement on standardized tests.

The implications of the cultural transmissionist/technical metaphor of the school for improving teaching are clear. Preservice and inservice efforts at educating teachers would include a strong emphasis on subject matter (e.g., requirements that all graduates in teacher education have an academic major), along with a dose of the research findings relating specific teaching strategies to test scores. Of course, all this would be measured at graduation by a standardized test (such as the National Teachers Exam) and later confirmed by continued observation and measurement in the field.

In fact, the Center operates on just the opposite principle (see Chapter 5). Teachers are explicitly told there will be no follow-up observation or measurement of how what they learn at the Center affects what or how they teach once they return to the classroom. The transmissionist activities that typify the technical model, such as rote acquisition of information, mastery of cognitive routines, and concentration on information, are specifically proscribed at the Center. Although the Center does not explicitly identify itself as opposed to the technical model in general, clearly many Center alumni perceive NCCAT as a refreshing change from the numerous state-mandated programs based on the technical model. While teachers do not see the Center as an antidote to trends they largely oppose, they do find the Center an oasis.

A metaphor for learning that more clearly reflects the thinking underlying the NCCAT curriculum is found in Kohlberg and Mayer's exposition of progressivist thought (1972, pp. 347-361). For the progressivist, knowledge is constructed through interaction between mind and environment. This metaphor envisions learners as philosophers, engaged in constantly changing dialogue with teachers, *who in turn are learners themselves*. The product of that learning is measured through a "functional approach" combining interviews, tests, and a naturalistic observation method (1972, pp. 461-463).

Prakash and Waks elaborate a similar line of thinking with their concept of "disciplinary initiation" in which learners come to think of themselves as contributing members of a community continually constructing knowledge (1985, pp. 82-85). They suggest a "view of knowledge and understanding as inherently social or intersubjective, as taking place in institutional contexts (e.g., the community of scientists, the art world) in which individuals contribute to an ongoing evolution of ideas and standards" (pp. 82-83). Program planners at NCCAT consciously engage in an effort to provide an institutional context for teachers to think of themselves as members of just such a community. We seek to do so through invitations to outstanding teachers to join with scholars from the arts, sciences, and humanities in exploring interdisciplinary topics.

The standard seminars sponsored by NCCAT bring together a heterogeneous group of elementary and secondary teachers to explore a problem usually not related to their own specific teaching specialty or field. The explicit statement of a focal problem forms the basis for the seminars. As Prakash and Waks (1985) point out, proponents of the disciplinary viewpoint see excellence in teaching as "inextricably connected with the ability to understand and appreciate the world from a variety of disciplinary perspectives" (p. 83), a view shared by the Center, whose planning ranges over a wide realm of the arts, sciences, and humanities.

The Center speaks in a unique way to teachers in inviting them to become members of a special scholarly community. Teachers are not only invited to sit at the seminar table as equals with scholars from the disciplines, but they are also invited to return to the Center as teacher scholars, pursuing the study of an advanced topic in astronomy, beginning to write a novel of their own, or just reading in uninterrupted seclusion. Here again, NCCAT focuses not so much on a product—although publications and grants have stemmed from teacher scholar projects—but on the sense that teachers have of themselves as worthy constructors of knowledge and art. The significance of this approach to teacher renewal is illustrated by the metaphors of vocation, journey, and vulnerability employed by Dwayne Huebner in "The Vocation of Teaching."

> The fallibility and insecurity that accompany teaching have been covered over by the metaphors of teaching as a profession, as a technology or method, or as an activity of schooling. The search for a method or technology of teaching carries with it the false promise that better methods of teaching can be given to teachers to reduce their insecurity or vulnerability. Difficulties and struggles of teaching are assumed to be a result of inadequate method, not an inherent consequence of the vulnerability that accompanies a vocation. To use the metaphor of profession is to see teaching as a knowledge based activity. This assumes that teachers should be sufficiently well educated to cope with problems, that knowledge is a protection

against insecurity and infallibility—it is a protective armor. (1987, pp. 24-27)

The Center speaks to teachers' sense of frustration and impotency at the continued imposition of standards and strictures in curriculum and instruction that increasingly deny them the freedom to pursue teaching as a distinctively human calling, with all the associated vulnerability Huebner describes. Huebner (1987) perceives the empirical and scientific lore that has dominated thinking about teaching for most of this century as an illusory quest for panaceas, which obscures the true nature of teaching as a vocation. The Center responds by providing a forum for teachers in which they can explore their common perplexities, frustrations, and vulnerabilities, freed from the onus of having to learn about the latest teacher-proof materials, new curricula, and effective teaching strategies.

The philosophical roots upon which NCCAT programs rest emphasize the dynamic nature of knowledge—that human knowledge is in constant growth and transition. Seminars with a scientific focus emphasize both the expanding knowledge base fostered by science and the limitations of science in providing insight into the human condition. Chaos theory, the topic of one Center seminar, underlines the emerging view that even within the purview of science a vast domain of phenomena exists that is not predictable in the old Newtonian sense. As Huebner suggests:

> Reasonable doubt, openness, and journey are also necessary prerequisites in the sciences. The point is that inquiry, knowledge, and technical developments cannot do away with or cover over the built-in vulnerability of the vocation of teaching. If vulnerability is done away with, or rather covered over and ignored, we simply turn teaching into productive technical enterprise that is unresponsive to the people and context within which it happens. (1987, p. 26)

Huebner recognizes the loneliness inherent in detaching from the view that knowledge and science provide a shield of invulnerability around the teacher, and he calls for the creation of a community in which colleagues who share the view of teaching as a vocation can converse about the conflicts in which they find themselves immersed. Indeed, the Center is evolving ever more intentionally into just such a special community. Driven at first by alumni demands for continuation of the NCCAT experience, Center programs have continued to evolve into a more extended pattern. Formally, this means the complex array of programs described later in this chapter. Less formally, and perhaps more important, it means the continuing connections and support networks maintained by the alumni themselves. Phil Schlechty's remark that NCCAT chooses its programs "with studied indifference" (see Chapter 3) suggests indifference to topics that teachers find irrelevant to their condition. It is an attitude in deference to creating the kind of community Huebner describes, in which teachers can discover themselves as colleagues with a calling.

"Humans on Earth: The Blue Ridge Experience"

In this section I describe in some detail one of NCCAT's earliest seminars. "Humans on Earth: The Blue Ridge Experience" is a popular choice of teachers admitted to NCCAT, and it has been repeated often. I have chosen to discuss this seminar because it illustrates several significant and common features of NCCAT programs.

1. Many NCCAT seminars take advantage of our unique geological, ecological, and cultural setting in the southern Appalachians. This principle could be generalized to other sites. The Center for the Advancement and Renewal of Educators in San Francisco, for example, recently implemented a seminar based in Marin County that explored the complex and unique ecological issues of the Bay area.
2. NCCAT programs are continually evolving in response to inputs from several sources, including teacher evaluations and internal pressures for growth and change. "The Blue Ridge Experience" reflects several generations of incorporating improvements from the formative evaluation process.
3. "The Blue Ridge Experience" exemplifies in practice many of the principles Rud describes in Chapter 3 dealing with the rationale, particularly the significance of interaction, hands-on experience, and hospitality.
4. The field experiences and the excursion into the Great Smoky Mountains National Park are illustrative of a trend to base seminars on site at the Center, but to include opportunities to explore firsthand the topic being studied.
5. The faculty of "The Blue Ridge Experience" has been selected over time for their capacity to teach and learn interactively not only with the teachers but among themselves.
6. The interdisciplinary approach described by Rud in Chapter 3 is strongly evident in "The Blue Ridge Experience." This topic is

particularly amenable to an interdisciplinary approach, and the faculty takes full advantage of the opportunity; that is, in any given session all the faculty may be participating, rather than taking turns in presenting the view from their particular discipline.

Every seminar has a focal theme or "seminar question" around which the program is constructed. The following is the seminar question for "The Blue Ridge Experience": How have the interactions between human beings and their environment in the Blue Ridge shaped both the environment and the quality of life in the region? We try to avoid seminars that are simply surveys or overviews of some topic; we try instead to choose a question that will weave together many interdisciplinary threads. Seminars are designed to provide not closure, but experiences from which participants can begin to build understanding. We hope that participants will want to go on building answers to the question and developing new questions of their own after the seminar is over.

As seminar coordinator, I am responsible for the overall design and implementation of the seminar. The whole seminar team typically includes a coordinator, who is usually an NCCAT Center fellow; a seminar faculty chosen by the coordinator; and an NCCAT program associate, who oversees all the logistical aspects of the seminar.

Members of the faculty have all worked together before in "The Blue Ridge Experience." Most come from academic backgrounds at a variety of colleges and universities, but others, like Dwight McCarter, bring years of firsthand experience in the field to the seminar. All the faculty have a flair for the NCCAT style; they are used to being on a first-name, informal basis with the participants, and they emphasize an inductive style regarded as central to our rationale (see Chapter 3). This faculty is especially good at an interactive, interdisciplinary style among themselves. Several are present throughout the seminar, and they question and critique each other's presentations. Most important, the faculty members are clearly learning from each other, and the participants are well aware of that process. The teachers of this seminar are learners themselves.

I have chosen to describe "The Blue Ridge Experience" as it happened, following the chronology of the seminar schedule, and commenting on each segment of the seminar as it took place. I have tried to capture some of both the substance and the feelings that play significant roles in this seminar, and to give interpretive comments as well. No seminar is without flaws as well as successes, and I touch on both, as well as including some teacher comment from the formative evaluation.

Sunday, May 27, 1990

The San Francisco teachers arrive at NCCAT, a first for us. Joe Giovinco, director of the San Francisco Center for the Advancement and Renewal of Educators (CARE), and I have been working for a year to develop an exchange of teachers between San Francisco and North Carolina. Earlier in the spring, 11 North Carolina teachers went to San Francisco to join their colleagues for a seminar on environmental problems in Marin County. Now 11 San Francisco teachers are arriving at Madison Hall for a reciprocal seminar on the Blue Ridge. They will be joined later in the day by 10 North Carolina teachers. This exchange seminar series is a precursor to our global seminar program, discussed below.

At the orientation, Bruce McPherson, NCCAT Director, gives the San Francisco teachers, rested after an early morning arrival, a special welcome. He talks about NCCAT's origins, the role of former North Carolina Teacher of the Year Jean Powell in proposing the Center, and a bit about the Center's organization (see Chapter 5). Most important, Bruce emphasizes to the teachers that this seminar is a reward for outstanding teaching, that it is just for them, not for the superintendent or anyone else, and that there are no strings attached. He sets the expectation that many of the most important outcomes of this seminar will be the result of informal interactions between teachers.

Dinners at NCCAT are special. To underscore our respect for our guests, we try to serve decent food in a pleasant atmosphere. Seminars frequently include a night out at an outstanding country inn, and/or an opportunity to share in a community effort to make our own meal. "The Blue Ridge Experience" features a Cherokee meal at a restaurant on the Cherokee Qualla Boundary, and a mountain meal cooked at Madison Hall, dining experiences that enhance and complement the topic of the seminar.

In the evening Dan Pittillo, a biology professor who is one of the seminar leaders, gives a brief overview of the week's plans. He is interested in discovering what the teachers are expecting and in assuaging any apprehensions about scheduled activities. Dan establishes informality and interaction as primary modes of communication. The tone of the session establishes the beginning for our emphasis on hospitality.

Monday, May 28, 1990

Cyril Harvey, a geologist from Guilford College, begins the seminar in the morning. He is a master of the inductive approach. Cyril begins by distributing a variegated pile of rocks around the seminar table, asking each of us to disregard what we think we know about rock origins and speculate as though we were Thomas Jefferson. A piece full of shells first identified as from the bottom of Charleston Harbor turns out to be from Lexington, Kentucky. The table buzzes with good natured exchanges as we sort and exchange rocks, and Cyril questions and probes the nature of our observations and reasoning.

Cyril goes on to briefly recapitulate some history of geology, emphasizing Hutton's influence in initiating the belief that ongoing processes deep within the earth continually are creating new rock. The session ends with a discussion of the advent of plate tectonics and a description with simple illustrations of the processes that created both the Appalachians and the Rockies.

The second segment of the morning revolves around descriptions and discussions of the October 1989 earthquake in San Francisco. The San Francisco teachers are each invited to pair up with a North Carolina colleague to tell the story of their individual experiences of the quake and to assess their subjective impressions according to a United States Geological Survey (USGS) scale. Some San Franciscans are initially hesitant about reliving their fearful experience, but everyone finds a partner and the session begins. San Franciscans do want to tell, and North Carolinians are riveted by these firsthand accounts. An hour slips by with anecdotes, questions, answers, and occasional tears. Cyril asks for the scale analysis of the event; we conclude that the official USGS tally is low by the experiences we have shared. The real seismic event of the day has occurred in this room; the two groups disappeared as such, and from this point on one seldom saw San Franciscans or North Carolinians sitting together as a group.

Following a rainy picnic lunch, we take a botanical walk across campus with Dan Pittillo, stopping to discuss the native and exotic species and their particular adaptations or vulnerabilities to the mountain climate. Showers and thunder hurry us along. Some members of the group lag behind while others forge ahead. It is difficult for everyone to concentrate on what Dan is saying.

The weather will challenge us again for the second part of the afternoon. Power goes down, and Dan's slide presentation on the historical ecology of the Blue Ridge is delayed. Slide shows are in ill repute generally at the Center, not so much because of technical glitches, but because they foster didactic teaching styles. Dan has mastered the technique of using slides to initiate questions, and when the power comes back on we explore the historical relationship of plant communities to the changing environment of the Blue Ridge, an especially significant background for later field experiences.

That evening Emily and Doris, black teachers from San Francisco, want to talk about the lack of black representation on Center staff and among North Carolinian teacher participants in the seminar. I explain that we do seek and are pleased when we get black applicants for NCCAT positions and that two of our current staff are black. The black community in this area is very small, and blacks are not particularly attracted to apply for positions.

The distribution of teachers as seminar participants is determined by their choices, as well as by efforts on our part to provide distribution by other demographic factors. We consciously try to mix teachers from across the state and from a range of teaching specialties, minority groups, and grade levels, but if no minority teachers rank a given seminar as a choice, we won't force that choice. Surprisingly, perhaps, the most underrepresented group at NCCAT seminars is the male teaching population. Twenty percent of North Carolina's teachers, elementary and secondary, are male, but only about 12 percent of our applicants are male. All-female seminars are not unusual; the three men in this seminar are from San Francisco.

Emily also wants to know why we are having a section of the seminar on the Cherokee without a Cherokee presenter. She is a teacher of multi-ethnic social studies units and would like to meet some authentic sources of material and ideas. Emily is right. I phone Laura Hughes, who teaches Cherokee language at Cherokee High School, and invite her to join us for dinner Tuesday.

Tuesday, May 29, 1990

Anthropology professor Anne Rogers begins the day with techniques similar to Cyril's in leading us through the prehistory of the Blue Ridge. She has artifacts for us to investigate firsthand, building ideas about how the people of the Archaic, Paleolithic, and Woodland periods developed relationships to the Blue Ridge distinctive to their periods, beginning more than 10,000 years ago.

Anne is highly skilled at drawing people into the presentation, so that although facts and principles are being learned from the body of archaeological research, it seems that we are participants in the process, rather than onlookers or passive recipients.

One of the more perplexing problems in staffing seminars is finding presenters who are comfortable with an interactive style. Despite all protestations to the contrary, occasionally a presenter just cannot get out of the lecture mode. Some seminar coordinators are expert at helping to shift gears, and participants can change the tone of the seminar themselves, but a few presenters persist in didactics. This usually shows up clearly in the seminar evaluation, and invitations to repeat these performances are not given.

Our field experience begins with a look at an ancient Cherokee fish weir in the Tuckaseegee River. A pronounced "V" of rock 50 yards long, designed to funnel fish into baskets, the weir is easily visible from the highway. Why hasn't it been erased by periodic flooding? We who live here have passed this way; Anne's eyes help us to see something we hadn't before.

A roadcut provides a geology stop. Cyril gives us eyes into deep time. The incredibly ancient contortions of the earth are written in striped scrolls that are clearly visible and touchable. No fossils here; this rock predates fossils, predates all but microscopic life. A billion years are recorded here: Time for the nameless ancient mountains that preceded the Appalachians to wear down and form these layers in Iapetus, the ocean before the Atlantic. Time for Africa to close Iapetus, crunching the North American Plate, giving rise to Appalachia, and in the process molding these same layers in swirled crystalline taffy tens of thousands of feet below the surface. Time for the Atlantic itself to open, and time for raindrops and floods and wind to wear down four miles of overburden. Deep time, indeed. We are awed. Billion-year shards find their way into our pockets and perhaps into future teaching.

Rain rejoins us for our picnic in the National Park. We delay our hike to the pioneer cemetery and head for the Cherokee Museum and its displays of the sad episodes of the Trail of Tears.

When we return to the Mingus Creek head of the trail for the promised visit to the pioneer cemetery, it is late in the afternoon. Misty rain still falls through the hemlock and rhododendron. I suggest that there is still time for a short walk, with a botanical emphasis, led by Dan, but that the hour is too late for the almost two mile walk up to the cemetery (and two miles back).

In our seminars, we aim to challenge at a level where our participants can experience success, not humiliation. Some of our teachers will attempt wilderness adventures in our "Why Wilderness?" seminar that they might not have under any other aegis. Still other seminar designers have developed aesthetic emphases, such as in "Freeing the Inner Voice," which invite teachers who would not otherwise do so to explore music, poetry, and dance.

Despite my suggestion, two teachers charge on up the trail toward the pioneer cemetery. I don't think they can make it in the two hours left before we are due for dinner, but, cynically, I decide to follow along just in case, certain they will turn back. They don't turn back. Forty-five minutes later we are at the cemetery, just as the sun breaks out over the flowering laurel surrounding the site. About two-thirds of the rest of the group is on its way up the trail as well, and they straggle up and back as I rearrange the dinner schedule. This is not as we had planned it, but those who made the hike are feeling proud of their accomplishment in meeting this physical challenge.

The day closes with a Cherokee dinner. We enjoy delicacies such as chestnut bread and bean bread. Laura Hughes joins Emily at the dinner table and they engage in animated conversation throughout the meal. Emily learns of some resources available and asks me to establish further contacts.

Wednesday, May 30, 1990

Harley Jolley, historian of the Blue Ridge Parkway, arrives with dozens of books on the history and geography of the Parkway. He spins marvelous tales of the politics surrounding the establishment of the Parkway route. His anecdotes of the people of the Parkway are complemented by "Jack Tales" from the repository of regional folklore. Harley has seen the living history of the Parkway and he gives it vivid reality for us now.

Harley, Cyril, and Dan all provide commentaries as we drive the 40 miles of Parkway from Balsam Gap to the Great Smoky Mountains National Park. Everyone participates in the half-mile hike to the top of Waterrock Knob. The atmosphere is free of haze, and we can see range upon range in the distance. Spring flowers are still in bloom here. But death is here, too; this is our first encounter with the ghost forests of Fraser firs, killed by the combined attack of wooly aphids and acid rain.

A fellow visitor stops me on the trail and inquires about the group. He comments that it is uncommon to see a group this size step off a bus with smiles on all their faces, and even more uncommon to see the whole group take off up the trail. Something is very different from the usual tour group, he says. He is right.

We stop at the Oconoluftee River bank with Cyril, watching the river work. Some scramble down the bank to feel the chill of mountain water. We imagine eons of the process before us. We do mental arithmetic with Cyril to calculate how long it would take to wear the land down to its present state at half an inch to the year. We think it took 150 million years at that pace.

Crossing the crest of the Smokies at Newfound Gap we pause to hike a short way up the Appalachian Trail. Dan takes us into a high hemlock grove, where we enjoy the silence, the dark, and the ferns. A sedge grows here, and only here, in the Park. The Park is a world biosphere reserve; no place else is like it.

The Wonderland Hotel at Elkmont is pre-Park, turn of the century, a relic of the time when Elkmont was a bustling summer resort. Elkmont is in the Park now, but the Wonderland and a surprising number of summer homes are playing out their last 2 years of special leases. Then the bulldozers will come, the land will be reseeded, and in time the quiet of the forest will prevail again. There is bustle, some apprehension, and some confusion as we settle in. At the Center everyone has their own private room, but here we will share. Before long most of us are enjoying the predinner hour on the veranda.

The day closes with Betty Smith, teacher, scholar, and Appalachian musician. She enchants us with her beautiful soft voice, her mastery of the mountain dulcimer, and the haunting lyrics of mountain songs.

Thursday, May 31, 1990

In the morning, Dwight McCarter, backcountry ranger, joins us. He has led sessions for us before, making marvelous presentations about tree carvings, tracking, and, this year, Indian petroglyphs. The Blue Ridge region has numerous examples of rock carvings, of more or less mysterious origin and meaning. One carving depicts the dismemberment of people with European characteristics, an event confirmed in the journals of the DeSoto expedition. Anne and Dwight engage in animated discussion of the universality of cross and sun symbols. Everyone is involved; Dwight has an extraordinary sense of humor that adds much to the occasion.

There is then a choice between a strenuous eight-mile botanical backcountry hike and less strenuous bus and walk tours in the Cades Cove area. Most participants opt for the less strenuous field activities in geology and archaeology. After some discussion, the geological and archaeological activities are combined. We frequently make such changes in response to participant suggestions.

The botanical hike heads off four and one-half miles horizontally and 2,500 feet vertically up Blanket Mountain. The group will follow Jake's Branch from its junction with the Little River to its source at Jake's Gap, passing through most of the major forest community types in the Park. From Jake's Gap a final half-mile push through rhododendron leads to the summit, a flowering meadow surrounded by laurel blooms.

The other activity runs into difficulty, a bridge that the bus cannot negotiate to get to the trailhead for the Cherokee Shelter Rock. The bus continues on to Wear Cove and makes a special trip to Cades Cove. The coves are geologic fensters, windows worn through the "overthrust" old metamorphic rock into the younger limestone below. More convincing evidence for plate tectonic theory. The coves are also fertile valleys, and Cades Cove has been preserved as a living museum of pioneer life in the Blue Ridge. A bear is sighted, and participants return to the Wonderland well satisfied with the activities, although plans were changed.

We return to Cades Cove for the night walk. As we arrive at sunset, another bear appears, on its way to the campground for an evening repast. The bear faces us and makes the preliminaries for a (Dwight says) "bluff" charge. Dwight charges first, snorting and gnashing his teeth, and the bear shuffles off. A lesson on dealing with black bears, but not for grizzlies. The rest of the night walk is a serene, lovely experience. As twilight fades numerous deer appear on the pasture land. Owls call softly. We end the day exhausted, but pleased with our experiences.

Friday, June 1, 1990

Friday comes, and with it an exploration of the world of the black bear. Our presenter is Mike Pelton, *the* bear man. He has been studying them for 20 years and has established an internationally renowned graduate program at the University of Tennessee in nearby Knoxville. Mike is accompanied by a graduate student from the Netherlands.

Mike's presentation brings together many of the diverse threads that have developed over the week of the seminar. He traces the evolution of the black bear into an animal admirably prepared to utilize the resources and to endure the rigors of the Blue Ridge environment. Humans have changed this environment, and bears continue to adapt, but the process is an uneasy one, especially in the interfaces between bears and humans.

Some of the major changes have occurred as a result of the introduction of exotic species and diseases into the region. The chestnut blight, brought from Europe, destroyed the primary food source for bears and many other forest creatures. The poorer diet of acorns is reflected in the smaller size of the bears. The introduction of the European boar into the environment has created competition in the same niche the bears occupy. Boars eat the same food, but they reproduce more quickly. Park rangers try to balance the situation by continual removal of the boars.

Interactions for humans and bears means trouble for both species. Bears are very intelligent and learn how to "panhandle," or to make backpackers drop their packs. Humans exacerbate the situation by feeding the bears. Mike shows us pictures of humans actually handing food to the bears. People are bitten and bears are transported, and the battle continues. National Parks are mandated to keep the land and its life forms in as primeval a state as possible and to make the Park accessible for the enjoyment of all. These are not easily reconcilable goals.

Mike offers us an opportunity to visit a bear den, only a half mile off the road. Most of us accept. The half mile turns out to be a quarter of a mile on the horizontal followed by a quarter of a mile of 70 degree mountain slope. We drag ourselves up by roots and tree trunks. Almost all of us make the trip successfully. We are soaked with sweat, muddy, and proud of our achievement. "No one, I mean no one, back at my school would have even tried this, but I did it," exclaims one teacher.

We close with a facinating hour watching Mike's graduate student scale a 90 foot oak to the bear den in the hollowed trunk, looking for a lost transponder. Mike and the participants continue the discourse, one question leading to another, becoming more aware of the extraordinarily complex relations among living creatures, including ourselves, in the Blue Ridge.

Following a mountain style dinner cooked for us by three women from nearby "Little" Canada, so named for its French Canadian settlers and the rigors and isolation of its high elevation locale, we begin the evaluation of the seminar. This process includes a written, scaled evaluation form and a discussion session devised with the assistance of the Learning Research and Development Center of the University of Pittsburgh (see Chapter 6).

Teachers evaluate our seminars with considerable candor, and, we believe, accuracy. They rate each individual session of the seminar, and they rate the facilities, services, and organization underlying the seminar. We value this formative evaluation highly, and we are convinced that it has much to do with the continuing improvement and quality control of our programs. After the confidential written evaluations have been compiled statistically, they are combined with written comments and circulated to the entire NCCAT programming staff. We also process the evaluations for their import in a staff session called "previews and critiques."

Participants rated 10 different parts of the seminar on a scale of 5.0 for highly effective through 1.0 for ineffective. Only one session rates less than a 4.0, the visit to the fish weir (which turned out to be mostly a glimpse out the window). Participants' comments suggest that they liked the sequencing of seminar discussion followed by field experiences; they were most disappointed when something about a field experience failed to meet expectations ("If you schedule a visit to a ledge, we should visit a ledge"), and most pleased when the field experience nicely complemented the discussion, as did the trip on the Blue Ridge Parkway ("The field trips were great, great, great!!! It so reenforced the classroom lectures. This reminds me as a classroom teacher to be more aware of this").

Written comments suggested a need for more accurate warnings about the difficulty of some experiences ("Please realize that a short hike means different things to different people"), and a stronger emphasis in the preseminar mailings about outdoor dress and footwear: "Tell people if they have boots to bring them. If they don't, buy them" or, "Be more specific about the endurance factors of the field activities."

Appreciation was expressed for the interdisciplinary nature of the seminar: "Why is it this way? Because of the geological history. Thus the relationship between geology and botany. I think I will be able to remember everything better because of the relationships that I was able to see between the areas" and, "All of the intellectual material placed in perspective gave each participant a sense of belonging and interrelationship."

Teachers were generally appreciative of the attention paid to the details of making the week an enjoyable one: "Everything from the warm greeting we received when we arrived to the toilet tissue in a [plastic bag] that Barbara gave us was a clear sign that you were interested in meeting our every need" or, "The atmosphere so warm, friendly, nurturing, and intellectually stimulating that one leaves feeling like a worthwhile human being again" and, "The pride of teaching has returned because of the wonderful way you said, 'Thanks.'"

On the merits of exchange, teachers from both CARE and NCCAT agreed that much was gained in understanding on both sides: "In comparing problems in San Francisco and North Carolina, I discovered problems are similar, people in the environment create the same problems and concerns." And they supported continuing such exchanges.

If it is fiscally possible, the exchange of teachers from San Francisco and North Carolina should be continued. Not only was this exchange professionally rewarding and enriching, it is also extremely enlightening. . . . Now I have a better understanding of my state in the total picture of the geological timeline. On a personal level, what a wonderful way to discover that though we live thousands of miles apart, we share common successes and problems at our schools and in our communities.

Finally, on the level of personal impact and future plans, teachers in this seminar expressed some important thoughts in terms of NCCAT goals: "I have so much to share with the students, teachers, and others when I get back. I hope to find some way to duplicate this experience, even if I have to plan it myself" or,

This experience was one of the most satisfying experiences I have ever had, and it truly is the richest professional experience of my career. I feel now that what I do is important and worthwhile. It is a boost that helps a teacher reach new heights (literally). I consider it a great honor and privilege to be part of this wonderful community.

Indeed we do hope that teachers who come to NCCAT will feel renewed, rewarded, and recognized for the excellence of what they contribute and that they will return from their experiences in some way determined to bring their renewal of spirit to their colleagues and their students.

Other NCCAT Programs

"Humans on Earth: The Blue Ridge Experience" is typical of one genre of NCCAT programs, the so-called standard seminar. Over the past 4 years, our programming has evolved into a complex array of (1) standard seminars, (2) teacher scholar programs, (3) special interest programs, (4) alumni reunions, and (5) global alumni seminars. In this section I describe significant examples of each type of program drawn from NCCAT seminar descriptions that are circulated to teacher applicants (Jones, 1990).

Standard Seminars

The standard seminar is the heart of the NCCAT curriculum. These seminars were the prototype programs introduced during the pilot sessions in the summers of 1985 and 1986 (see Chapter 2) and typically lasted 3 or 4 days, during which teachers in residence on the Western Carolina University campus participated in discussions of topics such as "Creativity, Leadership, and Change." The standard seminar is the first program for which teachers new to NCCAT are eligible, and more than 55 such seminars a year are held in Cullowhee. Following is a sampling of the range of topics that have been programmed over the past 4 years.

"Martin Luther King: The Power of a Dream" focused on the civil rights movement of the 1960s and on the life of its most revered leader. Seminar activities were held in Atlanta and included exploration of the art, music, and history associated with the movement. Emphasis was placed on the effect of the movement on growth and changes in an urban area of the South over the past 20 years. Seminar faculty included Hubert and Jane Sapp of the Highlander Research Center and other well-known Atlantans who were involved in the civil rights movement. Other seminars directed at the history and culture of minority groups include "The Tie That Binds," at Somerset Plantation, site of one the largest slave communities in North Carolina. That program explored the development of the rich heritage of folktales, dance, and music that created enduring bonds of fellowship within slave communities. "The Black Tradition in American Dance" looked at the masterpieces in dance created by great black choreographers and preserved by the American Dance Festival, and "Cherokee Nation: Beyond the Trail of Tears" explored the remarkable and troubled history and culture of the Cherokee, a nation within a nation.

Literature has been a recurring theme, as typified by "North Carolina Contemporary Novelists and the Art of Expression through Personal Experience," which was designed to investigate the development of the contemporary novel. Seminar activities included discussion of personal experience and its development into enjoyable literature and of the value of exploring one's past to enrich one's future. Novelist Clyde Edgerton and professor of American literature Mary Ellis Gibson led this seminar; other well-known writers at the Center have included Wilma Dykeman, Jim Wayne Miller, Kathryn Stripling Byer, and Lee Smith.

Music, like other Center topics, has emerged as a seminar theme primarily not for those who are experts, but for those who would like to learn about music, learn to perform a little, and perhaps even build their own instruments. "Freeing the Inner Voice: A Musical Exploration" was "designed for those who do not know how to read music . . .

to [learn] to read music through the use of the baroque recorder." In "Mountain Music" teachers learned to construct and play their own dulcimer. "The Revolutionary Beethoven" sought those who love both history and music to explore how Beethoven fit into the life, music, and politics of his time, and included an all-Beethoven concert performed by the Atlanta Symphony Orchestra.

Art has been the focus of "The Meaning and Wonder of Art"; within the supportive NCCAT context teachers who are not artists explored the meaningfulness and the history of art and analyzed masterpieces, supplemented by guided hands-on experiences. The visual aesthetic dimension was continued in "The Design of Earthly Gardens," which began with an exploration of landscape architecture through the work of Frederick Law Olmstead at the famed Biltmore Estate in Asheville and culminated in the actual planning and planting of a small "teachers' garden" at the Center (see Chapter 3).

Business and economics have received attention with "Economics USA" and "The Ethical Business Executive." Although these seminars too are designed primarily for the nonexpert, one edition of "Economics USA" was designated specifically for secondary economics teachers. The intent was to provide an opportunity for economics teachers to meet each other, learn about new research and tools in the field, establish common concerns, and begin a network, an opportunity not available to them through a regular professional specialty organization. A similar program was designed for secondary psychology teachers. "The Ethical Business Executive" brought together business leaders, academics, and teachers to critically examine common concerns and confusions over hostile takeovers, insider trading scandals, and bank failures, an example of an NCCAT forum for diverse, and sometimes opposing, points of view.

The environmental emphasis begun with "Humans on Earth: The Blue Ridge Experience" has continued in "Humans Versus the Environment: The Florida Experience," which takes place on site in the South Florida ecosystem. This seminar examines the severe damage to the delicate web of life in the most endangered national park, the Everglades, and goes on to survey the effects of continued overdevelopment of the Florida Keys. The effects of coastal development in North Carolina have been explored on the Outer Banks in "Graveyard of the Atlantic" through academic sessions at the Marine Aquarium and firsthand exploration of an estuary and its natural environment. The aesthetic awareness of nature is central to "Listening to Nature," as participants learn to appreciate the beauty, joy, splendor, and power of nature through techniques devised by Joseph Cornell.

A continuing thread in many seminars is philosophical discourse. "Our Founding Faiths: A Paideia Seminar" examines some of the seminal documents of American life and Western culture, including Plato's *Apology*, *The Declaration of Independence*, and Martin Luther King's "Letter from Birmingham Jail." Other seminars in this vein include "The Pursuit of Happiness," an exploration of connections between reason and imagination, self and community, and education and training through critical analysis of works by Goethe, Rousseau, and Mozart. "What is Love?" attempts deeper understandings of that profound concept through guided readings from Plato, Montaigne, Freud, and Marquez, as well as artistic activities.

International programming is a high priority. "Los Grandes Artistas de Espana" brings immersion in Spanish language study, old and new Spanish master painters, and exploration of Garcia Lorca's poetry, along with firsthand experiences of Spanish song by artist Teresa Radomski. "Into Africa" features African art at the North Carolina Museum of Art, African dance with Chuck Davis, and an opportunity to converse with African nationals. Other international topics have included "India: Contemporary Conflict in an Ancient Setting"; "Japan: Modern Miracle of the Far East"; "Oil, Islam, and the Middle East"; and "Escaping the Shadows: Mexicans' Quest for Identity and Survival."

Physical sciences and mathematics are areas in which NCCAT again tries to emphasize understanding for nonspecialists. One of the earliest such attempts, "Humans in the Cosmos," sought to explore the relationship between basic laws of motion and astronomical phenomena. The approach initially proved too esoteric for participants, but in the supportive atmosphere of the seminar, participants and faculty restructured the approach at a level that worked. Eventually a follow-up series of sessions resulted, called "Conquering Physics," which enabled the same group of teachers to continue to pursue the study of the laws of motion while observing themselves as teachers and learners in the process. "New Visions of the Cosmos," another astronomy seminar, emphasizes the ancient view of the universe, hands-on experiences with small telescopes, and present-day speculation about the origins of the universe and of life itself. "An Essential Journey through the Landscape of Mathematics" investigates the world of Gauss and Riemann, the evolution of mathematical concepts, and the linkage of mathematics with the real world. "Chaos" is an exploration of the discovery of chaos theory through recapitulations of the actual computer experiments designed by seminar presenters Ed Lorenz and Robert Devaney; it is unique as the first NCCAT seminar designed specifically for college faculty (teacher educators).

A final group of seminars is perhaps most commensurate with the needs for a special community described by Huebner earlier in this chapter and is primarily the work of Carolyn Toben, who has been associated with NCCAT since its inception. Toben's seminars have a strong emphasis on personal development and affect (personal communication, October, 1990). "Time and Remembrance" exemplifies this group, as the seminar descriptor shows: "This classic Center seminar will examine both culturally imposed and psychologically generated perceptions of time. Participants will seek through readings and experiential exercises to discover together the opportunities for breaking out of routine into the flow of creative thought." Other Toben seminars have included "Bridging Cultures," "The Magic Word," and "Child's Play."

Teacher Scholar Programs

Teacher scholar programs arose in NCCAT's second year from the recognition of a need for more unstructured situations for teachers who wanted to pursue their own intellectual and creative pursuits rather than attend a seminar on a predetermined topic. The first teacher scholar seminars emphasized group sessions on research techniques and grant-seeking skills, along with scheduled group discussions, meals, and other entertainment and social events. Teachers were admitted to these seminars on the same basis as to other seminars, and response was positive, but with a preference for even more unstructured time. In their current form, teacher scholar seminars offer time to exchange ideas if desired, mentors from the Center staff or Western Carolina University if desired, the resources of the university library, and some group recreation and entertainment. But the major priority is given to private time for individual inquiry.

Alumni of standard seminars are encouraged to apply for teacher scholar programs. They are also encouraged to design their own individual projects and to apply for NCCAT support and time to come to the Center to pursue scholarly and creative work in the arts, sciences, and humanities. Here again, NCCAT encourages teachers to think of the ways that are appropriate for them to grow intellectually and creatively, rather than urge that the product of a teacher scholar project be distinguished by publication or other outside recognition.

Teacher scholar projects have encompassed a remarkable range of pursuits. A teacher wanted time to pursue her interests in sculpture and was at the Center for 3 weeks in the summer, creating 51 works. Another teacher wanted time to begin a biography of her late, talented son. Still another writes poetry, composes songs for the guitar and voice, and relates all to computer education. For one teacher, time to read the poet Wallace Stevens uninterrupted for a week more than sufficed. A current project involves learning how to do astrophotography through telescopes available at the Center, with the advice of the resident astronomer at Western Carolina University.

Special Interest Programs

There is some overlap between standard seminars and special interest programs. Our initial experience with seminars designed for specific teacher interests, for example, in early childhood education, suggested that such seminars were counterproductive in the sense that teacher participants became preoccupied with narrow professional concerns rather than the overarching kinds of intellectual interests NCCAT wishes to foster.

Nonetheless, the Center has acknowledged the need of specific groups, such as secondary teachers of psychology and economics, for recognition of their special needs as relatively unrecognized and unorganized groups. Psychology teachers in North Carolina high schools, for example, are not extensively trained in psychology and can therefore experience feelings of isolation. There is no professional network from which to draw or colleagues with whom to exchange ideas and concerns. The seminar for high school psychology teachers aimed to bring this group together for exposure to new psychological theories and to share classroom experiences. Other special interest seminars have been designed for superintendents and principals to acquaint them with NCCAT programs, and for specific school districts to facilitate problem-solving processes.

Alumni Reunions

Alumni reunions were created to meet the consistent demand of NCCAT alumni for opportunities to continue the NCCAT experience. The reunions are held on a regional basis and typically last from Friday evening to Sunday noon. Although reunions may attract 150 or more participants, the NCCAT approach of informal discourse, discussion, and debate around the presentation of opposing points of view is maintained as much as possible. Typical reunion topics have included "The Perpetual Pendulum: Nature and Nurture in the 1980s"; "The Fourth Estate: Protector, Provocateur?"; and "Gun Control: A Hair Trigger American Issue." Reunions are designed to include presentations to the whole group, but a major part of the time is spent in breakout sessions. Ample opportunities are created for teachers to renew old ties and create new friendships.

Global Alumni Seminars

Global alumni seminars began in the summer of 1991 with "Oh Canada!," the first NCCAT seminar to take place outside the country. Global seminars are designed to expand the NCCAT experience for alumni of standard seminars who are interested in exploring a specific topic in an international context. A Global Seminar Advisory Board was established in 1990, composed of NCCAT alumni, NCCAT staff, a corporate contributions consultant, an international logistics coordinator, and business partners. This board suggested the following guidelines for global seminars:

1. Global seminars are modeled after NCCAT standard seminars in that they are designed around some focal question, topic, or theme, rather than designed to be tours.
2. Global seminars will be financed by some combination of teacher contributions, NCCAT support, and corporate contributions. One purpose of the corporate partnership will be to open comfortable forums for discussion between teachers and businesspeople.
3. Whenever possible, global seminars will provide opportunities to meet teachers in other lands and to begin to understand the conditions and meaning of teaching in foreign contexts.
4. The design of global seminars will emphasize different points of view and will not be influenced by the interests of any of the financial contributors. The final design of a global seminar will be part of the regular NCCAT programming process.

Projected global seminars in addition to the one in Canada include ones in Alaska and Costa Rica on environmental issues. A seminar planned for England will emphasize English literature, with on-site discussions of the works of selected British authors. A seminar in Mexico will view the total solar eclipse from the Yucatan and explore the role of astronomy in the Mayan civilization. Strong interest has also been expressed for seminars in the Soviet Union and Japan.

Summary

NCCAT programs have evolved into a unique curriculum designed to support teacher renewal. The standard seminars that are the foundation of the curriculum are interdisciplinary individually and across the entire span of topics. Both the substance and the style of the seminar curriculum stands in sharp contrast to more traditional notions of teacher education and development. The strong emphasis on individual construction of knowledge through interactive experiences with knowledgeable faculty and firsthand experience of phenomena being studied differs fundamentally from the traditional notion that knowledge is transmitted from teacher to learner. Perhaps most significant, the NCCAT curriculum is evolving from the notion of a one-time reward for outstanding teaching to a continuing relationship within a special community in which teachers are learners in a supportive, interactive context.

References

Dewey, J. (1956). *The child and the curriculum.* Chicago: University of Chicago Press. (Original work published 1902)

Huebner, D. (1987). The vocation of teaching. In F. Bolin & J. Falk (Eds.), *Teacher renewal: Professional issues, personal choices* (pp. 17-29). New York: Teachers College Press.

Jones, S. (1990). *Seminar descriptions and schedules, 1986-90.* Unpublished document, North Carolina Center for the Advancement of Teaching, Cullowhee.

Kohlberg, L., & Mayer, R. (1972). Development as the aim of education. *Harvard Educational Review, 42*(4), 449-496.

Prakash, M. S., & Waks, L. J. (1985). Four conceptions of excellence. *Teachers College Record, 87*(1), 79-101.

Chapter 5

Administration for Human and Organizational Growth

R. BRUCE McPHERSON

Little is new under the organizational sun or moon. In 1938 Chester Barnard threw a bombshell at readers of his *Functions of the Executive*, arguing that authority is granted to leaders *by* followers, and not the other way around. Yet how different is this from the nineteenth-century British politician Disraeli's comment: "Am I not their leader? Do I not walk behind them?" And did you know that Disraeli borrowed his one-liner from Seneca, the Roman Stoic philosopher? And did Seneca read, "Of the best leader, we will say, when our work is done, we did this ourselves," in the writings of Lao-Tse? Thus, when the phrase *shared leadership* is used in this chapter, it is done so with modesty and a sense that what goes around comes around, in the lives both of people and their organizations.

All of which is to say that while the North Carolina Center for the Advancement of Teaching is a renewal organization (not a large pond), and a state-funded renewal organization (a still smaller pond), and a state-funded renewal organization maintained almost exclusively for the benefit of outstanding K–12 teachers (virtually a puddle), it is not theoretically or operationally unique. Singular, perhaps, in some ways, but not firstborn. As a consequence, the avid reader of organizational literature will not find flashing new insights in this chapter. Those who have organized and managed and led NCCAT have stood on many familiar shoulders.

What can be said, then, to avoid completely dampening the reader's interest in these next few pages? Several things, I believe. First, formative and summative evaluations conducted for over 4 years indicate that NCCAT has been very successful in accomplishing its goals. In short, the organizational format and operational strategies of NCCAT apparently have supported programmatic efficacy. Such success stories are few, and they are worth attention. Second, and related to the first point, NCCAT has been almost narrowly client-centered. "Whatever Lola wants, Lola gets!" sang the star of the Broadway musical, *Damn Yankees*, and at NCCAT every employee knows that what the teacher wants, the teacher gets. NCCAT is accountable, and worthy of attention on that score. Third, NCCAT has been able to remain organizationally flexible. Having its own Board of Trustees and a special reporting relationship to University of North Carolina general administration offices in Chapel Hill (rather than, for instance, to trustees or officials at Western Carolina University, where it is housed) has permitted NCCAT autonomy and sanction in making rapid organizational adaptations to changing circumstances. Public administrators often draw water from dry wells in these regards. Fourth, and finally, NCCAT may be of interest because it has downgraded its reform role and emphasized, somewhat self-consciously, the renewal aspect of its mission. Renewal organizations require different internal structures than reform organizations. For instance, renewal organizations thrive on response to client needs, while reform organizations dictate client change. As a consequence, a renewal organization must have structural mechanisms to support quick flexibility and responsiveness. These matters just are not as high a priority for a reform organization. In this regard, formative evaluations are more significant for a renewal than a reform organization (which depends more heavily on summative assessments). Further, renewal organizations (unlike reform organizations) model behavior. If a renewal organization is promoting collegiality among its clients, it must be structured as at best a modified collegium. NCCAT has tried to be "the very model" of a collegial learning organization for the continuing benefit both of clients and staff.

I will refer to these particular attributes of NCCAT—efficacy, accountability, flexibility, and modeling—as we examine, in the following pages, several dimensions of administration that I associate with human and organizational growth. Intentionality will be identified, if and where it existed. Good fortune and blind luck will be noted in due course. Error will not be sidestepped. But few claims for originality will be made.

It Happened One Morning

I climbed the steps of Madison Hall (the renovated dormitory that was the temporary home of NCCAT) and walked across the second floor to the kitchen to find a cup of coffee. It was 7:45 A.M., but I knew that our lead housekeeper, Connie Wikle, would have several pots ready for pouring.

Full paper cup in hand, I began to walk gingerly through the seminar room. Normally, I would have heard the sounds of Connie's sweeper, but today she was leaning on it, looking up at a pair of large watercolor paintings over the upright piano.

Hey, Bruce, come on over here.
Sure. What do you need, Connie?
Look at those paintings. I think they're up there backwards.

What we were both looking at were two portraits of musicians. I knew that they were part of a set of four by a North Carolina artist that had come to us in a larger gift of art from the North Carolina National Bank. A cellist and a violinist in this duo. And, to be certain, the violinist was positioned with his back to the cellist. They seemed to be playing separately to two unseen audiences, rather than together and to us.

You're absolutely right, Connie. Here, let's fix them.

She helped me lift the heavy, glass-enclosed paintings down from their hooks and then reverse them. Ah, yes, the result was satisfying. We could almost hear the silent harmony as we stood there quietly for a few seconds admiring our handiwork. Then, without much more conversation, we moved ahead into our day of work.

I have recalled and replayed this scenario in my mind dozens of times, and I have told the story to others almost as often. It continues to uncover for me the crucial elements of administration for human and organizational growth. *Collegiality* involves respect for a good idea, from whomever. Connie, the housekeeper, saw something that Bruce, the director, to say nothing of those who hung the pictures, had missed.

Connie is a proud mountain woman, one whose work is respected by all her fellow workers. But what did she know about string players in their tuxedos and black ties, I wondered? She was not a chamber music devotee, I was certain. But Connie knew what was right, in the sense of right fit. Musicians who sit next to each other play together, regardless of locale or tune. Why want to correct the error, though? After all, she had not made it, and (apparently) it was not bothering others. What Connie was expressing was a sense of wanting all things harmonious, not simply those included in her domain by some filed-away job description. She knew of the NCCAT fetish for client-centered behavior. This was the teachers' seminar room, and something was awry, however subtly. The inclusion of original art in the seminar room, as well as in all the individual sleeping rooms that Connie cleans and arranges, is an institutional value at NCCAT. She felt comfortable initiating change in the realm of values. Her sense of responsibility here was as much moral as practical. In some way, she had been delegated *moral responsibility*, and she exercised it.

Are there also some insights, in this casual incident, about NCCAT as a *learning organization*, a place where the staff can grow professionally? As a student of my own environment, as well as chief myth purveyor, it is obvious that the incident was laden with meaning for me. For Connie, I am not sure. I never asked her, and undoubtedly I never shall. She will laugh if she ever reads this account. I can hear her now: "I was just trying to get things straightened up." Perhaps Connie is right, that it is just another simple incident in a day of work. But perhaps we are both correct.

Commitment in organizations usually is a tangle of sacrifice, nurturance, and exchange, and such was the case here with Connie. Two people encountered each other. A problem was identified and solved, and, in the process, commitment was uncovered and extended by employer and employee. What is even more interesting, however, is that collegiality and responsibility (moral and mundane) were the *vehicles* of commitment. If there is a tie that binds at NCCAT, it may be commitment. It is an idea that I shall return to at the close of this chapter.

Collegiality

A *collegium* is a group in which each member has approximately equal authority. A *colleague* is an associate in a profession. Thus, *collegiality* is a situation in which a group of fellow professionals govern themselves by sharing authority. One might expect to find collegiality in the midst of a *college* faculty, but, unfortunately, often that is the last place where it thrives. Collegiality exists at NCCAT, perhaps not in the pure form suggested by these definitions, but as one of its most important organizational attributes. Let us begin with some examples.

Our staff meetings (once and often twice each month) include all our employees. Graduate assistants may be in class, and our housekeepers usually are preparing for the Monday afternoon arrival of a group of teachers, but we try to get everyone else around the seminar table. The sessions tend to be longer rather than shorter. We form the agenda by going around the table and giving everyone a chance to make an announcement or ask for assistance or review a practice or policy or share information. We assume that thoughtful and clear communications when we are together face-to-face will save future time and prevent future confusion.

Other meetings tend to be open to those who have a need to know and have the time to attend. And we often "add" people to a meeting in an impromptu manner when we realize that their expertise is needed in order to come up with the best answer.

We establish flexible work schedules for colleagues who need them, including compensatory time for those who have worked evenings and weekends, regardless of role. Those who are pregnant or recuperating from serious illness or attending college courses receive such consideration.

Collegiality is not all peaches and cream. Identifying a problem is laudable, but sometimes collegial nerves are touched. At preview sessions, where a program designer exposes a draft of a seminar schedule to public scrutiny, no holds are barred. Criticisms and suggestions are not gloved, and feelings can be singed, for in the South controversy is worse than evil. Nor do we pretend at NCCAT that things are going well when they are not. When there is a budget crunch, budget summaries are distributed around the table, and implications of the problem are clarified for one and all, in dollars and cents.

We have adopted and sustained a collegial model not because it is a pleasant way to work with each other (which it is), but rather because our client-centered strategy demands it. We can not produce the "seamless" week-long seminars that both staff and visitors value without it. In the early days, one Center fellow (program designer) and one program associate (program logistician) were responsible for each seminar. Today, there is still a single Center fellow, but the program associate *team* works on each seminar. The group discovered that it could do a better job, and do it more easily, by supporting the lead program associate throughout the week. The team decided that on its own. The director was not consulted.

Also, we consciously model collegial attitudes and practices for visiting teachers, hoping to encourage them to build and strengthen similar contexts in their schools. NCCAT is very much part of that fabled real world; it is also an example (for our visitors) of professional life as it can be lived.

For teacher participants, there is an unusual opportunity to build a collegial group from scratch. The seminar group each week comprises between 18 and 22 teachers from all eight educational regions in the state—women and men, blacks and whites, veterans and relative beginners; from kindergarten through twelfth grade and a variety of disciplines and classroom assignments. And yet, with all this diversity, strong collegiality is engendered within several days. As an Asheville teacher observed, "We came as strangers. We left as friends and colleagues."

NCCAT teachers find that a diverse colleague group is an ideal *learning* resource. They come to realize that their group comprises *educators* who share many common interests and concerns that often are obscured back home by the grade level and school level assignments of teachers. Such newfound collegiality can persist. We have many reports of the reunions of NCCAT seminar groups, as well as ingenious systems of periodic communication to keep networking alive.

We are no longer surprised by the weekly blossoming of teacher collegiality. Many teachers *are* surprised, especially those for whom this condition is and has been in short supply. But even if we anticipate its arrival, we are no less affected by it. Teacher collegiality reinforces staff collegiality. It is a reciprocity that too few organizations enjoy, and it is one that we relish.

What can an administrator do to promote collegial values and practices in an organization? Collegiality can be modeled, of course. Its myths can be framed and circulated; its presence can be rewarded. And yet it is what the administrator does to change the organizational infrastructure that is even more important.

There are numerous examples at NCCAT. Special projects such as formative and summative evaluations, the teacher scholar program, and art acquisition bring unusual staff groups together over extended periods of time. An active written communications system permits a wide and effective sharing of ideas, questions, and information. Travel opportunities within the state (particularly to implement weekend alumni seminars) involve virtually all staff who are interested. And we mentioned earlier the matters of role flexibility, key information sharing, and staff meetings. These building blocks of collegiality at NCCAT are created not by fiat or policy pronouncement, but rather by ad hoc (organic, if you will) procedures. An opportunity arises; it is converted into a reality; and that reality is shared within the organization as stimulus to replication or variation. Administrative action is deliberate, but it is also spontaneous.

NCCAT is a collegial organization rather than a family organization (McPherson & Rinnander, 1988) where authority may be benevolent, yet still paternalistic or maternalistic. We prefer not to refer to ourselves as a family where everyone knows who is in charge, who the parents are and who the children are. In a collegial environment, authority is more provisional. To be sure, I make many "final" decisions at NCCAT. But respect is spawned by work and productivity rather than prerogative. In a collegial environment, planning becomes more natural and more predominant, and it involves many inhabitants of the organization. This planning process at NCCAT is one of the chief ways in which the spheres of autonomy of colleagues are expanded. Staff members are literally and figuratively drawn out of their offices into the larger flow of events.

There is evidence in our early history of the creation of a collegial life at NCCAT. I operated from several basic premises in the summer and autumn of 1986. First, the structure of the organization would need to insulate the design process. A flat organization was envisioned that would give me close contact with programming. Thus, three staff positions either were discarded, revised, or not filled. Bureaucracy was exchanged for collegiality.

I can hear my gentle reader saying, "It doesn't sound like collegiality to me. It looks like the director wanted more control and power." Such was not my intent. I realized that I was the only experienced administrator in the group. For me, quality control was a priority, as well as a position from which to help my colleagues learn our trade quickly. This was to change in time. NCCAT now has an assistant director, and we are less flat. But in our early years, it was important for me to be a working colleague as well as a boss, to share the core work at NCCAT—designing and implementing renewal seminars.

Second, a planning process was created prior to the opening of the Center that would ensure a long-range perspective on the development of individual seminars and clusters of seminars. The design process (from seminar idea to final evaluation) would be entrusted to the Center fellows. Within a year, programs were in place for a year in advance. Further assistance was provided by a detailed checklist, developed informally during the pilot period and then revised, expanded, and standardized. In this manner, long-range planning became a routine of internal organizational life at NCCAT.

I began to build an organizational structure that was collegiate as well as collegial. The Center fellows were considered as faculty members, with the usual prerogatives. I acted as a dean. In addition to seminar design and coordination tasks, all faculty were encouraged to engage in scholarly activities. As a consequence, a substantial number of papers and articles about the Center has been produced during its first 5 years of life.

I attempted to ensure that at a minimum two common understandings would draw upon and add to such collegiality. One was allegiance to what had been termed (prior to the operating period) as the Three R's of NCCAT—recognition (or reward), renewal, and retention. The best teachers in the state would be identified and praised publicly; they would enjoy a week-long seminar in Cullowhee; and, hopefully, they would continue to teach in North Carolina for many years. Most NCCAT employees can recite these Three R's. A second understanding was a sense of common responsibility for service to visiting teachers. From the teachers' perspective, it is pampering; from the staff vantage point, it is detailed and immediate hospitality. The person who carries the bag is the one who is at hand; the person who drives to the store to buy a bottle of aspirin for a teacher is the one who fields the request.

Perhaps the most telling evidence of collegiality at NCCAT is our reluctance to produce an organization chart. You would find none on the office walls at NCCAT. Seymour Sarason (1972) once observed that an early sign of organizational malaise is the urge (on the part of the leader) to revamp the organization chart. At NCCAT, the same might be said about the *creation* and *distribution* of an organization chart. In a collegial organization, the organization chart not only misrepresents working relationships, it hinders their growth and change.

In our collegium, my authority is reduced, but my contact with the organization is increased. I continue to be accessible. It is hard to tell if this can persist as NCCAT grows. Perhaps, inevitably, it will become more bureaucratic, less family-like. But it should do so reluctantly.

The Delegation of Moral Responsibility

Authority does not wake up administrators at 4 A.M. Responsibility does. The lack of authority makes the work of the leader more difficult, builds burning resentment, drains creativity. Responsibility is more complex. Events and stacks of paper can be overwhelming even to the veteran, but it is a sense of responsibility for what the organization has done, what it is, and what it will become that brings perspiration to the administrator's brow. It seems that one is in charge of everything from the purchase of paper clips to the annual report for the governing body. Tough work, when you finally get it. Do leaders have a franchise on leadership skills? If you believe that leadership skills are rare, you must try to control (uncontrolled) employees. If you think leadership skills are reasonably common, you will share leadership tasks with (disciplined) colleagues. At NCCAT, I have chosen the latter approach, and it is one that seems to suit a renewal organization. Why? At NCCAT we want staff not only to respond to client need, but to persuade the rest of us to do likewise if the response "works" in a seminar setting. It is the difference between efficiency and effectiveness. Leaders want both.

If the organization is to grow and prosper, work must be delegated. But what work, and to whom? *Routine work* is most easily given to others. Little control is relinquished; employees process assignments without very much imagination and investment, and wonder what the boss will want next. If more trust exists, then *authority and responsibility* can be delegated. The leader is saying, "This portion of what we do is yours. You have my support, at least until I begin to think that you're not producing." The delegation of a section of the organization is made with some asterisks that are apparent, and some that are not. This relationship is the norm in many educational organizations, especially as they grow larger.

Sometimes the leader is prepared to delegate *moral responsibility*. Organizational participants are empowered to help decide the character of the organization and its direction. Connie Hanna, a program associate at NCCAT, seems to be moving freely in this realm. As we chatted, I asked her:

> *What are the values that you think motivate those of us who work at NCCAT?*
> Well, respect for people, regardless of their position. And, then there's a way of operating that's beyond flexible . . . it's . . . openness, I guess. . . . We're not locked into a certain way of doing things. We don't feel we have to have things figured out in advance. Also, we have a sense of a better world, of what education can be. We don't cram learning in; we let it come out. And maybe one more. We include people in things.
> *How about outside NCCAT? What are the values that we express away from home?*
> Is there any difference? We take what's inside outside. I never thought about there being a dividing line. We can put our values into practice wherever.
> *I hadn't thought about it quite that way.*

You know, I came to work here because I believed it was a worthy task, what NCCAT is doing. And I see now that we pick people who fit that mission.
Do you sense any problems with the way we use our values?
We confuse reality with the goal sometimes. What they told me NCCAT *is* when I was being hired is really what we *want* it to be. But there's nothing wrong with that. We really do hit the mark most of the time. We are hierarchical sometimes, because we are in an academic setting. But, there's a lot of trust here. That's another important value. It's rare that someone lets you down. We all come from the old world.
Old world?
In contrast with the new world. It's not just NCCAT. Things are moving differently now, all over. The leader has to let go of all that control. And feminine values are allowed free rein here. You let that happen.
Maybe our society is becoming more androgynous.
The society is becoming more feminized. We allow our feelings to come into play, and they are accepted and encouraged here. It's a better balance all the time.

If Connie is correct, that is, if key NCCAT values are expressed internally and externally with relative ease, it suggests that service providers and clients are on the same moral wavelength. This is especially important in a renewal organization where initiative must come from (in our case) the staff and not the teachers. She speaks, too, of feminine (not necessarily feminist) values and their importance in the operation of NCCAT. Many of the men at NCCAT know how (or have learned how) to appreciate and extend "feminine values" such as an emphasis on intimacy and a consideration of the needs of other people, and tenderness as a public value.

Leadership is shared at NCCAT. The independence of the program team (Center fellows and program associates) is legendary. There are checks and balances, imposed collegially, but academic freedom and designer autonomy really are respected. Secretaries figured out the telephone system for the new facilities, and Sandy Hardy, another program associate, led the art acquisition project. Shared leadership—it has a nice ring, but is it enough for the leader to give up?

The delegation of moral responsibility cuts even more deeply into traditional organizational patterns. Colleagues are asked to share not merely in work, however significant, but in determining the worth of that work and the virtue of the organization itself. Let's go back to Connie Hanna for some examples.

- *"It's rare that someone lets you down."* Barbara Oglesby meets the teachers at the Asheville Airport at 11 P.M. on Saturday and brings them across the mountains, to be in bed by 1 A.M., so that Walt Oldendorf can take over late Sunday morning when people stir again. Literally hundreds of incidents such as this forge the value of responsibility and the expectation of its expression.
- *"We don't feel we have to have things figured out in advance."* This is not to suggest that advance planning is rare at NCCAT. Quite the contrary, it means that in the planning process innovation is expected to meet teachers' needs precisely. The evaluation of the basic teacher seminar over a 3-year period provides dramatic evidence of creative planning, as ethical, creative, experiential, reflective, and aesthetic components were added one by one. The NCCAT staff learned, sometimes slowly, to match design to need.
- *"We include people in things."* New hires are completed through search committees that virtually make final decisions. It is an obligation that is widely shared. A secretary served on a recent search committee for Center fellows; that was not accidental or unusual. Is this decentralization run amuck? Has the director abdicated? I would argue to the contrary. It is one of the ironies of organizational leadership that what goes around comes around. What you relinquish, you receive. The delegation of moral responsibility leads to an investment of staff in an organization that is exciting and exacting.
- *"The leader earns the authority to lead in return."* He or she may be hired to lead by a governing board, but that means little until there is staff ratification of the decision. People who do not want to be led will not be led. People will be led if they are tangled up (in ways not always discernible) with the moral leadership of the organization.

Problems, like weeds, crop up in an organization operated in this way. For example, flexible schedules and overtime assignments lead to compensatory time allocations. There is some abuse of this privilege at NCCAT. The value of perfection in planning and implementation also is strained simply by increasing programming levels. Independence and collegiality require a brand of self-discipline that must be learned, especially by citizens of what Connie Hanna termed the "old world." But in a renewal organization, independence and collegiality are more important values than goal setting and decision making, and are the

98 A PLACE FOR TEACHER RENEWAL

attributes that we want so much for our teacher guests to see and understand and take home with them.

The Learning Organization

It is beyond irony that educational institutions tend to be poor learning environments for educators. Many of the staff who joined NCCAT knew this in their bones; but far from discouraging them, negative experience only prompted determination to create a consistent and effective learning organization. There are many stories that could be told, but this is only a section of a chapter, and three will suffice here. The first (and longest) tale is that of a long-range organizational task involving many staff; the second reveals an aspect of the work of our seminar designers; and the third measures organizational learning in individual terms.

My work is crucial in the area of human resource development. While there are many ways to view, interpret, and understand collective life in organizations, my bias lies in the direction of the management of problems—the recognition, definition, and resolution of perplexities and dilemmas, large and small, crucial and mundane (Getzels, 1979; Getzels & Czikszentmihalyi, 1976; Kolb, 1983; McPherson, Crowson, & Pitner, 1986; Schön, 1983, 1987). But I am influenced also by theories of learning from experience. Kolb (1983) says: "The experiential learning process consists of four phases: concrete experience, reflective observation, abstract conceptualization, and active experimentation" (p. 112). This characterization can guide us here.

I have most impact at the stage of *concrete experience*, refining problems and pointing out directions that I feel are related to organizational effectiveness and survival. "Do this rather than this. Think about this before that." *Reflective observation* involves causal analysis of problems and scenario creation. "What happened?" "Why did it happen?" "What are some ways it might be ameliorated or solved?" *Abstract conceptualization* involves, at least for us at NCCAT, both intermediary problem solutions and the development of more general hypotheses. *Active experimentation* at NCCAT has taken place primarily in the areas of recruiting, curriculum, and organization. You weld theory to practice and then begin the four-step cycle again.

An organization starts with certain overriding, *given* problems. They are not concocted by the service providers or the clients of the organization; they result, more typically, from the necessity of and the imperative for action. The leader may enumerate or elaborate these

ADMINISTRATION FOR HUMAN AND ORGANIZATIONAL GROWTH

given problems, but generally they can be felt and understood rather easily by most of the staff of a small organization.

NCCAT began with three given problems.

1. How can we persuade teachers to come to the Center for renewal seminars?
2. What will we do with and for teachers when they are at the Center?
3. How will we organize ourselves to answer the first two questions?

Granted, these questions are too large, too vague to solve directly. Smaller problems had to be formed within what Dewey (1933) would call indeterminate situations. But these larger questions were starting points for action.

Let us turn to the first of them. In August 1986, this given problem had a time limit. By mid-October, groups of teachers had to be assembled for a series of seven autumn and early winter seminars. And there were no names in the pipeline at that juncture. For the pilot seminars in the summer of 1985 and in June and July of 1986, Teachers of the Year from schools, districts, and regions across North Carolina had been invited. The screening and selection had been done, in effect, elsewhere than at the Center. But a broader net would have to be used now. This was really the fourth stage of a cycle from the pilot period, *active experimentation* that had yielded important but insufficient guidance related to teacher recruitment.

The director and the teacher services coordinator chose four subproblems to focus their work in this area.

1. What should the application form be?
2. With whom should we make contact?
3. How should the screening occur?
4. What materials should we share with prospective clients?

These are not particularly profound problems, but they were the ones that it was believed had to be solved for the organization to expand teacher recruitment. The first stage of experiential learning—*concrete experience*—had begun again.

Two basic application strategies could have been incorporated in the application form itself. A short form of few demands might yield many applications (not an unattractive option at that early stage of organizational development), but also many rejections. A longer and more stringent form might produce fewer applications but also fewer rejections. The director had no desire to unleash a barrage of negative messages from the Center on the teachers of the state. Thus, the combined values of high standards and positive responses led to the selection of the second alternative and a form that included a substantial review of one's professional development history, two short essays, and two references (one from a teaching colleague and one from a supervisor). It had and has a reputation of being one of the most demanding applications for North Carolina teachers. The form has been affirmed over the years by both our alumni and marketing advisors for its emphasis on self-selection and for separating teachers involved in a serious search for renewal from prospective vacationers. Some 90 percent of teachers who complete the arduous application form are accepted.

In the past only superintendents had been used as nominators. A decision was made to mail an application and related materials to all of the 2,000 principals in the state as well, and to Center alumni. Three years later, these latter two groups had become the prime recruiters for NCCAT. It was also determined that the screening of applications would be handled collectively by the director, the Center fellows, and the teacher services coordinator. A proposal for a grass-roots, statewide screening procedure was deferred until the rate of applications called for its use. It has not yet been implemented. Finally, the need for a brochure was evident; the public information coordinator was asked to deliver one quickly, and he did so by Christmas of 1986.

The application form had been drawn up, a screening process determined, and a brochure designed and printed. Many more recruiting-related problems were found and solved (or at least ameliorated), which will not be reported here. It is more germane to the present topic to discuss the overarching experiential learning theory, and more precisely the second stage of *reflective observation*. Some of the results of that reflection are found in an unpublished paper by McPherson and Shapiro (1987), titled "Into the Mountains: Lessons from Veteran Teachers." The two individuals who had drawn up the application were responding (almost exactly a year later) to this rhetorical question: What lessons have veteran, exemplary teachers taught us about what they really need in the way of professional development? Five lessons were enumerated.

> Teachers want their minds to be stretched—by ideas rather than simply schemes for the better lesson plan. They want to argue without fear of recrimination or arousing hostility. They want col-

league networks that stretch far beyond their own schools. They want to be able to express their honest feelings with new friends and colleagues. They want to sit on the front of the airplane for once. These are the lessons that teachers who come to the mountains have taught us, and we are building our programs around what we have learned and what has been affirmed, week after week. (p. 14)

While this was quite positive, other reflective observation in the area of teacher recruitment was distressing. The number of seminars was expanding faster than the demand from teachers. Evaluations indicated the astonishing success of the seminars, but the waiting list was short and each recruiting effort, with its distribution of information and application materials, was only maintaining a current balance between programs and participants. The director and other staff were nervous because the reason for a low level of applications was unclear. Something more needed to be learned.

And thus a period of *abstract conceptualization* became prominent in 1988. We hypothesized that the problem was the stringent application form, but we were not certain, especially when alumni told us to maintain it as is. We felt some more objective advice would be useful, and we turned to a management consulting firm with experience in this area. Placing themselves in the shoes of NCCAT teacher clients, our advisors came to a position that could be summarized this way:

Your application form is excellent. Don't make more than minor modifications in it. But the materials you are sharing with potential participants are either drab or overpowering. You leave out a step—getting teachers excited before you hand them an application. So, produce a new brochure that is short and full of affect rather than boiler plate. Have teachers call in on your 800 number for an application. And how about giving them a chance to pre-register for a seminar? Now you only permit them to choose a seminar *after* being accepted. Maybe you have it backwards. And how about some mass mailings?
    But don't change that application.

The best advice often leads you away from your preconceptions. A new marketing approach based on enticement rather than assurance was emerging.

A period of *active experimentation* began in late 1988 and continued into 1990. A more attractive brochure was quickly developed.

Packets of information were adjusted to include materials for *both* the ready prospect and the potential prospect. A direct mailing was sent to all teachers in two counties—one dominated by a major city and the other in an isolated, rural part of the state. A pre-registration process was established. The application was edited but not changed in any important way.

What we have been describing is organizational learning writ large, the management of a critical function over time. But other groups and individuals have been inquiring and experimenting, too.

The Center fellows, the teacher services coordinator, and I began to organize a 6-month seminar schedule in the fall of 1986, and by July 1987 we projected seminars through June 1988. These culminating planning meetings took place in June and December. Monthly, the Center fellows met separately. These sessions were less effective, too often characterized by spats and tangential agendas. About the same time, we were learning to preview each seminar and critique it (after formative evaluation data were available). In contrast, a lot of learning was occurring in these sessions, even though they were sporadic, but they were not related to the bimonthly staff meetings or the Center fellows' meetings.

Learning how to learn in this sector began when a new Center fellow, Christine Shea, arrived. She argued for a revised seminar planning process that would not be a last-minute affair, but would involve discussions every month in Center fellows' meetings. When her colleagues agreed, their meetings opened up to all others involved in seminar design. Personal issues began to be addressed elsewhere. Then it was decided to have previews and critiques in a standard way on Tuesday mornings before the Center fellows' meetings. When program associates expressed a need for time to meet as a group with the Center fellows, a monthly session was scheduled for Monday afternoons after the all-staff meetings (reduced now to one each month). This has permitted the first Monday and Tuesday of each month to be devoted to planning (and learning) meetings. Attendance is not required, but the practice is something close to that. Experiential learning is not quickly achieved. This format took 3 years to evolve. It feels comfortable, but it will continue to change.

When Laura Bishop, our budget officer, expressed her frustrations over finishing her undergraduate degree on a night school basis at WCU, I suggested that she go full-time for a year and end the malaise. Others made the same suggestion, I am sure. So, Laura went to school by day for a calendar year and completed her B.S. in criminal justice (14 As and 1 B). She worked part-time at NCCAT on a schedule that changed every week. She simply notified her colleagues each Friday of her availability the following week, and there was nary a ripple. Incidentally, Laura was not trained as an accountant when she came to NCCAT. We needed someone to handle the budgets; she was available, and she learned how to do the job.

Recently, a program associate said to me, "I thought everyone had the right to learn here." The *right* to learn.

Commitment

The eternal problem for any organization is to find a balance between the interests of the person and those of the group. For the administrator (and perhaps most especially for the nominal leader of the organization), it is important to position oneself to see that this exchange between the one and the many is mutually effective.

Reference to Jacob Getzels's (1969, 1978) model of social behavior in a social system is useful here. Getzels argued that two dimensions must be considered. The first is the *individual* dimension, for the organization comprises people who have various personalities and exacting needs and dispositions to act in one way as opposed to another. But there is, at the same time, an *institutional* dimension, for the organization is characterized by roles for which there are formal and informal expectations. And, Getzels emphasized, the two dimensions are *interactive*. They create (through both conflict and harmony) the reality of social behavior in a given human organization. There is an ebb and flow between each organizational inhabitant and the collective that varies over time, and it is this counterpoint multiplied that begins to describe the complexity of organizational life.

Where does the administrator take a primary stand? With the organization? Some do, as they attempt to bring personal needs and dispositions under the sway of role expectations. It is the goals of the organization that take precedence for these men and women. With one's colleagues? Others find this posture more comfortable, and they spend their time bending the organization to meet the individual's agenda. Here the objectives of participants, one by one, have first priority. Still others take a middle course, arbitrating between the organization and the individual, sensing that the best outcomes are those that satisfy both employer and employee. Of course, such pure types of administrators exist only rarely. My point is that leaders (like trees in the winds of the mountains) have their tendencies.

At NCCAT leadership has tended to be of the latter variety. In an entrepreneurial organization like ours, the dream has been a happy staff and happy clients. To the extent that the dream has been realized, credit must be given to what Getzels calls transactional leadership— committed to both the organization and the individual, co-opted by neither, motivated by a desire to find compromise and (better yet) consensus, and sobered by the moral edge of such responsibility. McPherson, Crowson, and Pitner (1986) have observed that Getzels was

> uncomfortable with the administrator as a company man or as a maverick, and he opted for a posture of mixed allegiance. What Getzels is asking the administrator to do is to make a tough moral decision. He knew that the rewards for the established company man or for the established (or occasionally undiscovered) maverick are more predictable and durable than they are for the administrator in the middle who runs the risk of attack from every side and, even more probably, isolation. It takes courage to pursue a course as a transactional leader, with the loneliness, disappointment, and delayed recognition that accrue. But, suggests Getzels, it is the correct direction. . . .
>
> The administrator cannot permit the organization to wander (or even perish) as a result of unbridled conflict. The school organization often represents the interests of a governing board which is particularly sensitive to the financial interests of clients in the organization context. Yet the organization also represents a custodian who is concerned about the quality of medical insurance which is protecting his family. The trustee *and* the custodian need never meet, and for the most part they do not care about each other's possibly disparate goals. But the *administrator* must know both, and he or she must negotiate between the two, advancing and mediating the needs of the trustee and the custodian. (p. 345)

One way to think about commitment in an organization is to consider direction. How does commitment *flow* between the individual and the institution? Kanter (1968) described commitment as sacrifice, moving largely from the individual to the organization. Etzioni (1961, 1980) saw commitment as exchange, with an interchange resulting from negotiation. Porter and Miles (1974) were among the first to portray commitment as nurturance, initiated by the organization and flowing toward the individual. Once again, these are types, and hardly so pretty and clear in real life. But, we suggest, they are observable. An interview with Margaret Rose Simon, a program associate, yielded such evidence.

What kind of sacrifices do you make to work at NCCAT?

My job involves working outside the normal work day. There's no question I have to be away from my family more than I'd like to be. Those extra costs for babysitters on evenings or weekends are not easy to meet, either. Next, I would probably make more money in another position, but I feel that I need to get the kind of experience here that will lead me to that well-paying job later. And then the vacations—I never seem to find time for a good, long vacation. The last thing is the work I have to take home almost every night. Two hours, usually. It comes from the extra projects I take on, and I want to get the job done and done right. Yes, there are some sacrifices.

In contrast, are there ways in which NCCAT seems to reach out to nurture you without your asking for help?

The flexible schedule and hours. That's so important for many of us. And the open door policy; you really have access to the leader. I also respect the "take care of your own" policy at NCCAT. And to be given a chance to grow—the ability of the organization to let you learn from your mistakes. That's always there, it seems. NCCAT is willing to teach you the things that you need to know to be successful. Then you can use your skills.

NCCAT fosters interdependence. It has taught me the use of *we, our,* and *us* rather than *I, my,* and *me.* I positively shudder when someone uses the *I, my,* and *me* vocabulary. That's too independent.

Some things an organization gives you are like an exchange—a paycheck for work completed, for example. How does this occur for you at NCCAT?

I get a pleasant working environment, one where there's a tolerance of disagreement; an openness to the other way; a receptivity to new ideas. NCCAT helped me find my career direction, what I want to do. It's so clear now. The path, the support, the supervision are all there.

What does NCCAT get from you?

I give my best. I mean I give 150 percent.

Have you made a dent or two on the organization? On its values, or policies, or procedures?

Yes. Particularly on our buildings. I really influenced most of what went on in setting up this place. And I've been just as involved in planning for and decorating our new facilities. I haven't made any policies, but I have developed procedures, such as our checklists, and alumni reunions, and large-scale purchasing. What I really love is to help many teachers make their connection with NCCAT very positive. I ask to do the reunions, even though they are away from the Center and my children, because it's so gratifying to work with our alums again.

When you feel that closeness and intimacy and laughing and crying, you know the purpose and mission of NCCAT has been reached. I help do that. In some small way, every time, I help do that. What I do makes a difference. I love what I do. It's hard, and you can't fake it.

For Margaret Rose, the opportunities to learn how to do her job well and to find a career direction (conference and housing management) are major inducements for her cooperation. In addition, she exchanges hard work for a collegial working environment and being in a position to help teachers find meaning in their renewal experiences. In this latter regard, she is the purveyor (and occasionally the creator) of the values of NCCAT. The elements of sacrifice, exchange, and nurturance are all there, and for Margaret Rose really adequate pay is a deferred incentive at this stage of her career.

The administrator cannot do the work of the organization. I try to find colleagues who are willing to participate (to join the organization) and to be steadfast, to continue to participate. Incentives build commitment, and at NCCAT we have focused on incentive *systems*. That is, we have tried to alter the natural tendency in organizations for incentives to be controlled and distributed by the few and for the few. Staff throughout the organization are encouraged to be not simply learners, but teachers. As much as she may have learned from her stay at NCCAT, Margaret Rose is remembered especially for constructing and leading an intensive one-day socialization for new Center fellows. Groupings (rather than lectures) to promote collegiality appear naturally, as at off-site weekend alumni seminars, when typically the director, a Center fellow, a program associate, the public information coordinator, a secretary, and a bus driver work shoulder to shoulder. The delegation of moral responsibility is not left to chance. All employees are encouraged (over the course of a year) to work directly with teachers and visiting faculty in a seminar, even if only briefly, to stay in touch with the issues of service delivery. And, like Margaret Rose, many then find that they are not simply preparing lunch, but helping teachers realize their best dreams. These are collective processes in a renewal organization, not a function of the boss. Commitment encompasses collegiality, moral responsibility, and learning, and it is infused with meaning by all three.

Conclusion

Myths are important to an organizational culture. They tell its history in a colorful and memorable way; they cement its people together; they reveal its essence. By myth, I do not mean something fictional or fantastic, but rather the stories and themes that appeal to the consciousness of a group by giving expression to common ideals and feelings, to the group ethos.

Pieces of the NCCAT myth come from many sources (e.g., an alum's poem, simple data, actual incidents in the life of the Center, observations by staff from their experience in seminars, and staff-generated writing about the Center). I have taken the lead in collecting and polishing, while many of us do the sharing with our clients.

The myth-sharing process at NCCAT takes place at least once each week when newly arrived teachers are oriented to the Center. Typically, I speak to the group for one-half hour, just before the first supper meal together. If I must be absent, then the seminar coordinator plays the role of myth sharer, using notes that I have circulated several times (1987, 1988, 1989). These versions are roughly identical, suggesting that the shaping and recording of organizational myths were especially intense in 1986–1987, the first year of NCCAT operation. To be sure, some of the comments in these orientation sessions involve policy (e.g., the use of alcohol, smoking areas, public access to the Center, uses of photographs taken by staff, respect for sleepers late at night). Still, the majority of items portray the Center with regard to what it has become or ideally what it will become.

The myth has four essential themes. First, the Center conveys the gratitude of the State of North Carolina for the service of its finest teachers. NCCAT staff and programs are merely the vehicles for the expression of appreciation from the Governor and the General Assembly and the University of North Carolina. For teachers who rarely receive sufficient praise from their principals or school parents, this is a powerful, riveting idea. It is associated often with the Three R's, as in:

> The State is saying, "Thank you very much. You thought we weren't noticing, but we were. We appreciate what you have

been doing. This seminar is a way of rewarding you with a renewal experience. And afterwards, we hope you will go home and teach our boys and girls and young men and women forever. You are outstanding teachers. *You* hold our schools together."

A second part of the myth has to do with teacher presence in the Center. Jean Powell was a very special educator, North Carolina's Teacher of the Year for 1983-1984. At the beginning of each seminar, I read to the newly assembled group her testimony to the North Carolina Commission on Education for Economic Growth on November 29, 1983 (see Chapter 2 for text).

I do so to show that the *idea* for the Center came not from a politician, but from a teacher. Staff are introduced in terms of their teaching background (most have one). And stress is placed on matters such as teachers (three) and alumni representatives (two) on the Board of Trustees, artwork purchased from teachers, and the growing significance of alumni activities at the Center.

Third, the role reversal from teacher to student is stressed, usually through a story from my experience.

> I was walking upstairs when I was almost bowled over by a teacher I had not met before. We laughed and she apologized and continued past me.
> "Are you one of the teachers?" I asked.
> "No, I'm one of the students," she replied. She took several steps and did a perfect double take. "Oh, no, I'm one of the teachers."
> I knew then that the seminar was in good shape. She had become a student. She was letting things flow in a different direction.

This part of the myth helps teachers go through a transition from the world as it is to the world as it might be. Release from back home—its pressure and responsibilities—now is mirrored by release from a dominating professional role.

The fourth and perhaps the most important piece of the myth has to do with teacher control of NCCAT and its experiences.

> This is *your* Center, not ours. Use it fully. Explore its nooks and crannies. You'll find that it's a terrific place. You will enjoy the faculty, the presenters, and the fellows, but the greatest learning

resource sits around this table. You will learn more from each other than anyone else. We can control many of the logistics of the seminar. But only you can control your learning. Thus, you have the responsibility for telling us when adjustments are needed. Be candid rather than polite. Let's not waste your learning time.

A related statement that draws rapt attention and that is remembered across the months and years is this one. It lies closer to the heart of the NCCAT myth.

This seminar is for you. It is not for your students or your fellow teachers back home or your principal or your superintendent or your board of education. You do not have to take notes or make out a lesson plan or develop a report based on this seminar. This seminar involves learning for the sake of learning. This is for you. You have earned it. You deserve it. Relax and enjoy it. *And do not feel guilty.*

Teachers know that much of their professional development has been for the benefit of others. They savor the NCCAT difference.

A final reinforcer of the myth is a poem by Edward Milner, a high school teacher from Charlotte and an active NCCAT alumnus. It was read by the author at the ground breaking for the new NCCAT facilities in April 1988.

To the Center

> Teacher invited here, pilgrim and guest
>   Opens his heart, revealing division
> Between his mind and body. A shared rest
>   Seals integrity and refines vision.
>
> Sacred stress reminds him to confess
> His debt to you for wrestling with the same anxieties.
>
> A center is softer, can heal and bless
>   Despite vanities and varieties;
> So much richer in yield on the vast quest,
> Where truth, like holy shrine, becomes a sign.
>
> Annealed and restored, he finds him self blest
>   and ready to reenter the long line.

As ground is turned here, the soil is ripe like loam;
May learning build a habitation and a home.

Myth-making and myth-sharing at NCCAT energize the organization. The commitment to key ideas and goals is stressed. Collegiality is emphasized for staff and clients alike. The delegation of moral responsibility occurs in a public setting. And what the staff has learned from its clients is shared with new clients each week. The renewal organization is renewed.

References

Barnard, C. I. (1938). *Functions of the executive.* Cambridge, MA: Harvard University Press.

Dewey, J. (1933). *How we think: A restatement of the relation of reflective thinking to the educative process.* Boston: D. C. Heath.

Etzioni, A. (1961). *A comparative analysis of complex organizations.* New York: Free Press.

Etzioni, A. (1980). Compliance structures. In A. Etzioni & E. W. Lehman (Eds.), *A sociological reader on complex organizations* (3rd ed.) (pp. 87-100). New York: Holt, Rinehart and Winston.

Getzels, J. W. (1969). Administration as a social process. In A. W. Halpin (Ed.), *Administrative theory in education* (pp. 150-165). New York: Macmillan.

Getzels, J. W. (1978). The communities of education. *Teachers College Record, 79,* 659-682.

Getzels, J. W. (1979). Problem finding and research in educational administration. In G. L. Immegart & W. L. Boyd (Eds.), *Problem finding in educational administration* (pp. 5-22). Lexington, MA: D. C. Heath.

Getzels, J. W., & Czikszentmihalyi, M. (1976). *The creative vision: A longitudinal study of problem finding in art.* New York: John Wiley.

Kanter, R. M. (1968). Commitment and social organization: A study of commitment mechanisms in utopian communities. *American Sociological Review, 33,* 499-517.

Kolb, D. A. (1983). Problem management: Learning from experience. In S. Srivastva (Ed.), *The executive mind* (pp. 109-143). San Francisco: Jossey-Bass.

McPherson, R. B. (1987, 1988, 1989). [Director's opening commentary to NCCAT seminar participants.] Unpublished notes.

McPherson, R. B., Crowson, R. L., & Pitner, N. J. (1986). *Managing uncertainty: Administrative theory and practice in education.* Columbus, OH: Merrill.

McPherson, R. B., & Rinnander, J. A. (1988). Collegiality: Its meanings and purposes. *Independent School,* Fall, 41-45.

McPherson, R. B., & Shapiro, K. S. (1987). *Into the mountains: Lessons from veteran teachers*. Unpublished manuscript. Cullowhee, NC: NCCAT.

Porter, L. W., & Miles, R. E. (1974). Motivation and management. In J. W. McGuire (Ed.), *Contemporary management: Issues and Viewpoints* (pp. 545-570). Englewood Cliffs, NJ: Prentice-Hall.

Sarason, S. (1972). *The creation of settings and the future societies*. San Francisco: Jossey-Bass.

Schön, D. (1983). *The reflective practitioner: How professionals think in action*. New York: Basic Books.

Schön, D. (1987). *Educating the reflective practitioner*. San Francisco: Jossey-Bass.

Chapter 6

The Role of Evaluation in the Development of the Center

WILLIAM W. COOLEY AND WILLIAM E. BICKEL

Early in 1985, shortly after the state legislature mandated the establishment of the Center, a planning group under the leadership of Donald J. Stedman, Associate Vice President for Academic Affairs of the University of North Carolina, recognized the need to define a strategy for evaluating this innovative program. As they began the search for appropriate evaluation resources, Stedman contacted us, and as a result of that phone call we were invited to North Carolina to attend a meeting of the planning group for the purposes of learning about the plans for the Center and sharing our views about evaluation. We had just completed the manuscript for a book about decision-oriented educational research (Cooley & Bickel, 1986) that was based on our work with the Pittsburgh public schools, and we were eager to explore how this approach to evaluation research would work in other contexts.

The conversations about evaluation at that meeting were wide-ranging. Although most of the participants stressed the value of building in a program of evaluation from the beginning, there were lots of different views of what that evaluation should emphasize. One participant even wanted a study that would link teacher participation at the Center with higher student test scores! Others wanted to emphasize the Center's impact on improved teacher retention. In our discussions we emphasized the need to distinguish between formative evaluation, which would be designed to generate information useful to Center staff as they began program implementation, and summative evaluation, designed to generate information useful to others in thinking about the value of NCCAT. We pointed out the importance of starting with a strong program of formative research that would be useful in guiding program improvements as the Center evolved. Too often a summative evaluation is imposed on a new educational innovation before it gets well implemented. So we were asked to develop a design for formative evaluation, with the understanding that we would begin the summative evaluation after the program was well established.

There are several elements to decision-oriented educational research (hereafter DOER), and since they influenced what happened here, it may be useful to summarize them. One element is our commitment to taking a client orientation toward the development of the evaluation research agenda. For the formative evaluation, the clients were the program developers, and so we worked closely with Center staff as we designed and implemented data collection and feedback procedures. When we turned to the summative evaluation, the clients became the Center's board, key state legislators, and others who would participate in decisions regarding the future of the Center. Dialogue with such "significant" others determined the summative research agenda.

Another component of DOER is the use of an eclectic approach to methodologies for data collection and analysis. This recognizes the complementary nature of quantitative and qualitative data, and the need for both in determining how a program might be improved and or in appreciating the program's value. DOER also recognizes the need to establish computer-based data files, so that information about program and participants is systematically collected and organized from the beginning, and is available for timely and comprehensive reviews of the program. At the same time, DOER emphasizes the importance of program documentation, preserving and organizing both the "paper trail" of important memos, program descriptions, and so on, as well as in-depth interviews of participants so that the evolution of the innovation can be understood.

In this chapter we describe the procedures and substance of the formative and summative evaluations that were conducted for the Center from 1986 to 1989. We hope that in what follows the reader can gain additional insights into the nature and value of NCCAT, as well as how one might go about the task of evaluating this type of educational innovation.

Information for Shaping an Evolving Program

Defining the Formative Agenda

The initial contact between the program's leadership and the evaluators led to a series of telephone and written communications that shaped a program of formative research, to focus on the first three pilot test seminars in the summer of 1985. This dialogue between the researchers and the "client" identified three goals for the research, namely, the assessment of participants' views of

1. Their immediate, overall reaction to the experience
2. The value of specific seminar components that had been offered
3. How any aspect of the program (substance, structure, or operations) could be improved for future seminars

The early conversations between the program staff and the evaluators identified three basic data collection procedures to be used in the research. Members of the evaluation group would attend and observe sample segments of the pilot programs. A survey using both rating scales and open-ended question formats would be administered (initially in most instances by the evaluation team) to all participants at the close of a seminar. Finally, also as part of closing day exercises, the evaluation team (or a member of the NCCAT staff not directly involved in the specific seminar) would lead the participants in a focusing session designed to identify points of group consensus and disagreement about the program.

The goals of the observations were to acquaint the evaluators with the basic operation and spirit of the program and enable them to better understand and be able to interpret teacher feedback on written instruments. The questionnaire was designed jointly, with extensive interaction between program staff and evaluators. It continued to be shaped over time based on ongoing dialogue to improve the value and clarity of the data, and on changing program information needs that occurred as the program itself modified its efforts over time. All parties felt that it was important to have both short and close-ended response items as well as open-ended items on the instrument. This was partly to ensure rapid turnaround of analyses and partly to facilitate the development and tracking of quantitative trends over time, a particular interest of the board of trustees. In addition, open-ended questions were included that would allow teachers to record in their own words the meaning of the experience, its strength, and how it could be improved, and to provide insights about what a quantitative trend in the data might mean.

The group evaluation sessions started with two goals in mind and eventually added a third. First, they gave the participants a formal opportunity to voice their reactions and to hear the reactions of others to the experience—an opportunity for consensus or disagreement, which was instructive for participants in its own right, about the status of education and the profession in North Carolina. Second, they gave the evaluators an opportunity to be interactive with the participants—pressing home questions of clarification that simply could not be done with a written set of responses. Eventually, NCCAT administration suggested an additional function for these group sessions, namely, to elicit teacher input on broad policy issues confronting the Center (e.g., the best procedures for facilitating networking among Center alumni).

In combination, the formative evaluation strategies yielded a rich database on participant perceptions of the Center. These data were summarized for NCCAT leadership in several ways. It is important to note that how they were communicated back to the Center evolved over time in relation to the information needs of the leadership.

Initially, general summary reports were prepared by the evaluators. These were designed to provide the administration and the board of trustees with an overall portrait of the experience—what occurred and what participants thought of it in relation to the Center's original mission. For example, the first such report on pilot programs offered in the summer of 1985 addressed the following questions:

1. Who were the participants?
2. What did the teachers experience?
3. Do the teachers feel rewarded as a result of their experiences?
4. Do the teachers feel rejuvenated as a result of their experiences?
5. Does the teacher feedback vary significantly by session or by type of session?
6. What is the overall teacher assessment of the seminar?
7. How can the program be improved?

In addition, a supplemental report was prepared that provided some information on individual program components within sessions.

This general approach to reporting of formative evaluation data continued through the fall of 1986, with increased attention given to across-seminar analysis and comparisons of data and trends. However, by this time a number of things had occurred at the Center that would directly affect the nature of the formative evaluation process. A permanent director had been appointed. With year-round programming, the pace of seminar development had picked up considerably and could be expected to continue. Additional staff was appointed, with seminar design responsibilities distributed across more Center fellows. The evaluation exercise was affected in several ways.

Correspondence and telephone communication between evaluators and Center leadership clarified a number of concerns about level of detail and timing and resulted in specific changes in the structure of the evaluation. Clearly, the Center needed the evaluation to be responsive to at least two broad audiences. The macro summary reports of the type produced early in the process were valuable resources to NCCAT leadership in communications with the board of trustees, state educational leaders, legislators, and others. This level of documentation of activities and results served to inform these audiences of Center activity and functioned as progress/accountability measures for those responsible for Center funding.

A second type of information reporting was needed by Center staff and seminar leaders. These constituencies required considerably greater detail about each seminar than was previously provided by the evaluators. Further, such reports had to be done quickly. The Center was often in the position of having to make decisions about whether to repeat a seminar offering later in the same year and, if so, in what form (including what presenters to invite back). To meet this need for seminar detail, a second style of report was designed.

The additional report focused on each substantive component of a seminar. Quantitative data (frequencies, percent by response, means, and standard deviations) were provided on the teachers' ratings of the effectiveness of a speaker or activity. In addition, qualitative comments by teachers were reported. Response frequencies means and teacher comments that were formative in nature and of particular utility for improving the component were color coded in the document.

The emphasis on reporting formative data from teacher commentary reflected the information interests of NCCAT leadership. Invariably they found these data to be of greatest interest and most helpful in modifying the program. The seminar-level reports were issued as quickly as the data could be summarized, eliminating the lag time that necessarily occurred with the macro reports across seminars.

Having data does not ensure that data will be integrated into the decision processes of a program. Regular NCCAT staff meetings were held to review the reports as they were issued. The data from teachers were added to the staff's own perceptions of whether a particular seminar or an activity within it had gone as intended. In combination, teacher data and staff reflection provided a strong basis for influencing program structure and content. Both methods for delivery and the substance of what was delivered were continually shaped by the flow of formative data to the program's leadership. Several examples of types of formative feedback garnered from teachers through the research process are provided below, using information drawn from evaluation reports on 1987 and 1989 seminars, respectively.

Qualitative responses on teacher questionnaires administered during the winter and spring of 1987 indicated that approximately 17 percent of the teachers wanted more unscheduled time in seminar programs. The open-ended responses indicated that such time would be useful in permitting teachers to engage in more informal, integrative discussions about concepts being presented in the formal sessions. Further, they sent the signal that dynamic teachers, used to being on the go within their classrooms, found it difficult to sit for lengthy periods of time within the seminar setting, no matter how stimulating the material.

Teachers gave specific suggestions for seminar topics that the Center might consider in the future. Again, using 1987 data, topics ranged from a consideration of educational reform concepts like the "Paideia proposal," to a consideration of American dance and its influence on our culture, to the study of North Carolina's Native American heritage, to teacher as writer, to the study of physics through a variety of hands-on experiences.

Summaries of teacher data from 1989 winter/spring seminars indicate that the most frequent suggestion for improvement concerned offering the opportunity to return to the Center with one's original group. Additionally, participants continue to be a rich resource of ideas for future programming. Folklore/storytelling, western North Carolina heritage, archeology, jazz and blues music, and teachers—the retirement years are examples of topics suggested by teachers participating in 1989 programs.

The central point to be made here is that a strong program of formative research systematically enabled participants to play a key role in shaping the ongoing direction of the program. It modeled in a specific, tangible manner a central principle of NCCAT, namely, a deep respect for the profession and the quality of the intellects of teachers, a principle quite different from the staff development approach that tends to apply a remedial model to teacher development efforts.

Transferring the Formative Evaluation Function

By the second full year of the Center's operation, the basic structure of NCCAT was well established. This structure included the multifaceted formative evaluation process described above. While particular questions would change, the essential components of the research process were in place. Both the evaluators and the program's leadership had envisioned from the beginning of the relationship that the formative mission would eventually be fully integrated into the NCCAT operation, that is, be conducted by Center staff. This transference of formative functions was felt to be important for a number of reasons.

Formative research is best done close to the program under investigation, by those most knowledgeable about the program. The planned increase in the pace of program offerings would necessarily make it difficult for an evaluation group based in another state to maintain the on-site contact that is important to the analysis and interpretation of teacher data. The expense of observing and conducting evaluation exercises would have been prohibitive. Further, turnaround time is necessarily slowed by having instrument preparation and analysis functions located away from the program. While the practical issues are not trivial, the most important point to be made is that deep understanding of the intent and the experience enhances the capacity to fine-tune instrumentation and to understand and interpret the perceptions of others about a shared experience.

Groundwork for transferring the formative research function to the Center began in 1987. NCCAT personnel came to Pittsburgh and worked with the evaluation team on reviewing all phases of the research process. Computer compatibility was established. A member of the NCCAT staff received training in relevant software and in various data analysis procedures. The establishment of a computer-based data file has been particularly helpful in the institutionalization of these formative evaluation activities. For example, Center staff are now in a position to keep excellent track of their alumni, and in the future they will be able to work up their own demographic descriptions of the teachers they are serving and where, for instance, additional recruitment might be needed.

Provision was made for on-site follow-up at the Center. In addition, a member of the evaluation team served as an ongoing consultant to Center staff as they established the database on site. The Center's staff was in a position to begin producing the seminar-level reports by early 1988. They produced the first macro report across seminar sessions by the summer of that year. The basic structures of these research efforts and reports continue today.

Issues of Long-Term Program Impact

Developing the Key Questions

As we have noted, the evaluation plans for the Center included both formative and impact-related responsibilities. Another important reason for transferring the formative function to Center staff was the need to begin the design and implementation of studies that would generate information that would help others see the value of this type of center for teachers.

The process of defining the focus of the study of Center impact paralleled the conversations on transferral of the formative research program. The first step in the summative evaluation was to conduct interviews of people in a decision-making position with respect to NCCAT, such as state legislators, regarding their current perceptions of NCCAT and the questions they would like to see this evaluation research answer. As we noted earlier, this approach reflects a deep conviction that the results of evaluation research will be useful only to the degree to which the primary clients of the evaluation are involved from the beginning in establishing the important questions to be addressed. Our work points out the critical need for evaluation studies to be guided by the information requirements of people who are in a position to make decisions relevant to the program being evaluated.

Thus the priorities and specific designs for this decision-oriented educational research were guided by the outcomes of the client interviews. This allowed us to identify what people wanted to know as they sought to get a better sense of what NCCAT was and what it was doing to improve the quality of education in North Carolina. Those interviews were important in establishing the major questions to be addressed in the summative investigations. Different people may want different kinds of information as they think about the possible value of the Center. The interviews identified a wide range of possible questions that guided our evaluation activities. The questions included:

1. Who is the program serving? How are teachers selected and how are they distributed throughout the state, both demographically and by grade level and subjects taught?

2. What do teachers do in this program? How does the program work? What are the teachers learning?
3. How does this program relate to other state and national efforts of teacher renewal and retention? How is it unique? What justifies its uniqueness?
4. What evidence is there to suggest that teachers in North Carolina consider this experience a reward for excellent teaching?
5. What evidence is there to suggest that this program helps to retain excellent teachers?
6. What evidence is there to suggest that this program renews excellent teachers?
7. What does this program cost and how do these costs compare with other things that might be done to renew and retain excellent teachers?
8. Although the immediate reaction to the NCCAT experience has been very positive, how do teachers feel about the experience after a year or more?
9. Does this program have any impact upon North Carolina education beyond the teachers who have been directly involved? How can that kind of impact be extended?

The results of the interviews of key decision makers made it clear that what a summative evaluation might focus on depends on the kinds of information needed by the primary clients. The NCCAT summative research focused on questions 1, 3, 6, and 8.

NCCAT, Educational Reform, and Teacher Renewal

One evaluation task was to examine NCCAT in the larger contexts of national educational reform, as well as other statewide efforts to retain quality teachers in North Carolina. Important educational innovations such as NCCAT can best be understood by examining them in terms of those larger contexts.

One important development in the early 1980s was the work of Schlechty and Vance (1981), who studied North Carolina teachers and found that the most academically proficient teachers were the ones most likely to leave teaching. Their extensive investigations indicated that North Carolina faced a steadily deteriorating pool of academically talented teachers.

A more recent study of North Carolina teachers by Strauss and Sawyer (1986) showed why it might be important to be concerned about that type of attrition. They showed how teacher quality, as measured by National Teacher Examination (NTE) scores, was directly related to various measures of student achievement.

There were several responses to these and other concerns about the quality of teachers in North Carolina. There were calls to upgrade standards for admission to teaching and for paying more for the better teachers through career ladder and similar programs. Schlechty and Vance (1981) warned that "policies that attend only to selection criteria for teacher education programs may do nothing more than produce a teacher shortage" (p. 107).

What is so importantly unique about this NCCAT experience is the "R" that is missing—remediation. Most other reform efforts that have involved teachers have placed them in staff development efforts that focus on improving the teachers' skills (Warren-Little & Stern, 1988, for example, have documented this trend). Teacher renewal tends to be a remedial model, and the skills that are taught are often some latest enthusiasm for how to teach better. The NCCAT approach is to work toward the improvement of education by making sure the best teachers stay in teaching, have an opportunity to renew their "spirit" and their intellectual life, and feel appreciated for their contribution to society.

One of the concerns of teacher professional groups is the intellectual and professional isolation of the classroom teacher and the need to build collegiality among teachers. The evidence from this study of NCCAT makes it very clear that the seminars contribute much to reduce that isolation and to increase professionalism. Darling-Hammond (1989) has pointed out the importance of improving the status of teachers as we seek to improve education. Here again, NCCAT is making important contributions.

The NCCAT Teachers

It is appropriate to examine this educational reform in the context of the total state system. Toward that end, statewide data were obtained for all of the state's 58,000 teachers. Information included the usual demographic data: geographic location, sex, race, age, educational background, teaching career patterns, as well as current professional activities. In addition to these statewide data, through the previous formative evaluation activities a database has been established of all NCCAT participants. This enabled us to relate the characteristics of NCCAT teachers to the state's total teacher population through group comparisons. Before turning to those results it is important to understand how teachers are selected for this program.

Initially, teacher selection began with the local district administrators, who were encouraged to nominate their best teachers for this program. The next step was largely self-selection, in that teachers were asked to follow extensive application procedures. Ultimately, the final NCCAT selection committee screening process was more a matter of finding a good fit between teacher and seminar than it was of selecting or rejecting applications. Over 90 percent of those who completed the whole application process were accepted for an NCCAT seminar.

After the program had been in operation for a year, there was an important shift in the selection process. NCCAT alumni began to identify other teachers who they thought deserved and would benefit from the NCCAT experience. This initial peer nomination is important, since it combines a familiarity with the Center with a knowledge of which of their teacher colleagues would profit from the experience. This is very similar to the initial nomination process in such prestigious enterprises as the Center for Advanced Study in the Behavioral Sciences. The NCCAT selection process still requires local administrator support of the nomination, but it does not limit the initial nomination process to teachers considered by school administrators to be deserving.

Turning to the question of how the NCCAT teachers are distributed across the state, the answer is, remarkably well. For one thing, *every* school district in the state has had at least one NCCAT teacher. NCCAT staff worked hard at obtaining broad statewide participation. The one exception at the writing of the summative report on which this commentary on data is based, is the south-central area of the state, where teachers were underrepresented by 50 percent. (That is, 13 percent of North Carolina's teachers are from this area, but only 6 percent of the NCCAT teachers are from there.)

Another type of underrepresentation is in terms of males and minorities. Although 20 percent of North Carolina teachers are male, only 12 percent of NCCAT teachers are male. Similarly, while 20 percent of the teachers are minority, only 7 percent of the NCCAT participants are black or another minority. So while the Center is clearly doing well in attracting talented teachers from all over the state, as of the fall of 1989, there has been some degree of underrepresentation for certain categories of teachers.

The Follow-up Study

The main research task of the NCCAT summative evaluation was to survey the 740 teachers who had participated in NCCAT seminars between the summer of 1985 and December 1987. The main purpose of the survey was to get the teachers to reflect upon their NCCAT experience and describe the impact that the Center had on them.

As indicated in the formative evaluation data, the immediate reaction to the NCCAT experience was very positive. For the purpose of understanding the long-term impact of the Center, it was important to find out what happened when the teachers went back to their schools and how they felt about the experience after 6 months or more. Although the survey was conducted during the summer of 1988, we used participation prior to January 1988 as the cutoff because we wanted to ask teachers to reflect on their NCCAT experience and report what had happened to them when they went back home. It was important to have some distance between their seminar and the survey.

A common problem with surveys of this type is that the people who return the survey may be different from the ones who do not respond. This response bias is often positive in nature. That is, individuals who *do not* respond may be less successful, may have more to be reticent about, or may be more negative about the program than those who do respond. To check on this possible response bias we drew a random sample of 40 nonrespondents and made a concerted effort to find them (including follow-up phone calls). This special follow-up allowed us to conclude that there was no significant response bias, so it is reasonable to assume that the results that follow are true of NCCAT teachers in general, and not just the 60 percent who chose to respond to the questionnaire.

Part 1 of the survey instrument consisted of a set of six questions that dealt with the teacher's experience at the Center. These open-ended questions were then coded so that we could describe the main types of responses we got for each question. The following composite portrait emerged:

> The main reason that I attended an NCCAT seminar was the need for rejuvenation and intellectual stimulation, and that indeed was the best thing that happened to me at the Center. The chance to go to NCCAT was very definitely perceived to be an honor, and the most rewarding aspect was that the Center staff made me feel really appreciated. The most important benefit of the Center was the opportunity for renewal, and the intellectual stimulation provided by the fellow teach-

ers and Center staff was the main reason for that feeling of renewal.

In Part 2 of the survey the teachers were presented with several unsolicited testimonials that had been offered by some of their fellow teachers. They were asked to indicate the extent to which they felt those quotes were true of them. The overwhelmingly favorite quote was "The thing most admirable about the Center is its trust in teachers." The teachers felt that they were treated as intelligent, deserving, highly valued citizens, and teachers are not used to that type of treatment. Other high-scoring quotes dealt with: the rewarding nature of the good food and the physical setting (one teacher indicated that it was the first time in her life that she had a bedroom to herself!); the opportunity to form close ties with other teachers from North Carolina; and the fact that the Center renewed their love of learning.

What was also important in the quotes is that these teachers were *not* willing to describe themselves as "burned out." The portrait that emerges from the data is of dedicated teachers who love working with students. Their largest concern is about the conditions under which they are often forced to work, particularly the lack of time to reflect and plan. They very much appreciated the NCCAT hospitality and relaxed setting, but they also pointed out that it will be important to improve the conditions under which teachers sometimes have to teach if North Carolina is to keep its excellent teachers. As one teacher put it, "You don't volunteer to go to Vietnam because you heard that the R and R in Hawaii was great."

The third part of the survey dealt with what happened when they got back home. Eighty-five percent have remained in their same positions, and most of those who changed jobs simply moved to a different teaching job. The big difference back on the job was that they felt renewed, recognized, and more confident.

One very important side effect of this Center experience is the statewide network of talented teachers that is being established. Over 80 percent of the participants stayed in touch with their NCCAT colleagues and made new contacts with other NCCAT alumni not even in their seminar. An important bond is developing among these professionals; they are communicating with other professionals with similar interests and concerns; and they are participating more in other professional development activities. Many of those activities are self-initiated and self-directed, such as writing, fellowships, and graduate school. But they also very much appreciate the fact that the NCCAT staff is staying in touch and providing local seminars and other similar events. The data also indicate that the NCCAT teachers are assuming important leadership roles in their profession in North Carolina.

Part 4 asked them to think about their future, particularly whether or not they planned to stay in teaching. That kind of question, of course, is related to if and how NCCAT is having an impact on teacher retention. We have concluded that this is essentially an unanswerable question. For example, even if we determined that the retention rate for NCCAT alumni is 87 percent, while for North Carolina teachers in general it is only 80 percent, and established that difference for a defensible comparison group of teachers with similar ages, teaching experience, and other relevant demographic variables, there is still the great self-selection factor that cannot be statistically controlled. That is, we have established that NCCAT attracts a very dedicated, professionally oriented teacher, so any observed differences in retention rates could be heavily influenced by the type of teacher who applies to the Center, and could not be attributed solely to the Center experience itself.

Teacher Commentary

One type of evidence regarding the power of the NCCAT experience has been the unsolicited letters and comments that teachers have shared with the NCCAT staff, either immediately following their seminar participation or after reflecting upon it back home. The only problem with such testimonials from an evaluation research perspective is that it is not clear how representative those comments are. To test this, we took the testimonials that had been received and developed questionnaire items out of them in order to establish just how generalizable those claims were. As we indicated in discussing Part 2 of the follow-up results, most NCCAT teachers shared those opinions about the positive benefits of NCCAT.

In summary, and to further illuminate the value of the NCCAT experience to North Carolina's outstanding teachers, comments that are typical of those made by NCCAT participants are provided below. These are all direct quotes, and there are hundreds more where they came from. They are provided here because they represent important evidence about the impact of this experience on North Carolina teachers.

Other professions offer the opportunity to break away from the daily rut—teachers also deserve this out of respect and gratitude for their work. They deserve to be treated as professionals.

I needed time to work and think away from ceaseless demands of my job and family—I got it there!

The *time* to complete a goal, gave me a wonderful feeling.

I gained the realization that grants and publication opportunities are not just for the nebulous "other," but could be for me.

The scholar in residence program gave me a chance to carry through with a writing project that I wanted to complete.

I plan now to start some new research on the gifted child and on effective communication within the school community.

My level of awareness was raised. I had not been challenged to think nor did I have the opportunity to interact with interesting educators since graduate school.

My self-esteem as a teacher was boosted tremendously. I had begun to have doubts as to how much difference I can make. My seminar made me feel professional and inspired me. What I do is certainly important to the future of our world.

Concluding Comments

Evaluation research continues to play an important role in the ongoing evolution of the Center. Through the feedback loop initiated in the formative research exercises, the Center has a rich source of information on immediate impact and what can be done to further improve the program.

The summative research has established a clear basis for identifying NCCAT as one of the important educational innovations in the country today. The new wave of educational reform is focusing on the teacher. NCCAT is demonstrating in a very convincing way how to renew and reward its excellent teachers; the program is demonstrating how to establish potent, informal, professional networks among those teachers. Although it was not possible through the summative research to establish the direct impact of NCCAT on teacher retention, current studies of teacher retention are identifying factors that increase retention, and NCCAT seems to be enhancing those factors. More research is needed to demonstrate a direct connection to retention, but the renewal and reward goals of NCCAT are clearly being met.

References

Cooley, W. W., & Bickel, W. E. (1986). *Decision-oriented educational research*. Boston: Kluwer Press.

Darling-Hammond, L. (1989). Teacher supply, demand and standards. *Educational Policy, 3*(1), 1-17.

Schlechty, P. C., & Vance, V. S. (1981). Do academically able teachers leave education? The North Carolina case. *Phi Delta Kappan, 63*(2), 106-112.

Strauss, R. P., & Sawyer, E. A. (1986). Some new evidence on teacher and student competencies. *Economics of Education Review, 5*(1), 41-48.

Warren-Little, J., & Stern, D. (1988, April). *State teacher policy and local professional development*. Paper presented at the annual meeting of the American Educational Research Association, New Orleans.

Chapter 7

Learning from NCCAT: An Outsider's View

GARY A. GRIFFIN

This chapter is written from the perspective of an outsider, someone who is in many ways a "stranger" to NCCAT. I have visited the Center and have had non-Center professional relationships with one or two of the Center staff, but my perspective on the work and the vision of the organization is not embedded in the daily life of this new institution. In some ways, this is an advantage for the purposes of this chapter: I can become a stand-in for readers of this book and others who are concerned with the issue of teacher renewal. This chapter's content is the consequence of my own reflection upon what other authors in this volume have chosen to tell us about the Center. Their choices tell us what is important to them and how they interpret their own and others' NCCAT involvement. Rather than report, as is true for most of this book, this "outsider" can comment, infer, suggest, and speculate—rare opportunities for most of us who are fully occupied in the ongoing dailiness of getting our work done.

The questions that frame this chapter are both simple and complex.

- What can the experience of the North Carolina Center for the Advancement of Teaching tell us about working with teachers?
- What issues and concerns about teaching and teachers are addressed by the Center and deserve our serious attention?
- Why should we consider the NCCAT story as something other than merely another tale told by insiders of a particular organization?

With regard to the last question, I believe strongly that the early history of the Center gives us an opportunity to consider three important sets of conditions related to working with teachers. First, NCCAT's approach takes more seriously than is usual a number of important issues related to teaching and teachers. Second, the Center treats these issues imaginatively and coherently. Third, the curriculum, content, and process of the Center's work with teachers demonstrate a set of values and expectations that are sufficiently uncommon to provoke response. Each of these conditions will be discussed after a brief acknowledgment of the relation of the organization to its social and cultural contexts.

NCCAT and the Times

This book comes at a time when extraordinary attention is being paid to teachers, teaching, and schooling. The attention takes many forms and is shaped by many voices. From policy makers, we hear that tighter control of the enterprise holds promise for "improvement." Researchers tell us how to think about changes in schools and teachers (The Holmes Group, 1986). Formal and informal coalitions of concerned parties invoke various conceptions of "reform" as predictions and possibilities for altering educational practice (Carnegie Forum on Education and the Economy, 1986). Some of our citizens, both parents and others, express their expectations for teaching-learning settings in wide-ranging and sometimes conflictual frameworks—education for democracy, for economic growth, for personal satisfaction, for group cohesiveness, for individuality, for improved technology, for creativity. Teachers express confidence, sometimes uneasily, in opportunities to rethink the nature and surrounding conditions of their work (Lieberman, 1990).

At the center of all or almost all of these expressions about schools is some explicit or assumed notion of "teacher." To some, a teacher is or should be a technician, someone who has command of the tricks of the trade. Others believe that teachers and students will benefit if teachers are more reflective and analytic than is believed typical. Other views demonstrate the explicit conflict about whether subject-matter expertise or pedagogical knowledge is most important for excellent teaching. Some believe that teachers are best considered as objects of "reform," while a competing conception is that of teachers as members of a collegium whose responsibility is to come to grips collectively with ensuring best teaching practice (Griffin, 1990).

The common denominator for all of these expressions, and others, is the public faith that is placed on the importance of teachers, whether to guarantee the attainment of a societal goal, as in the case of "education and the economy," or to promote individual well being, as with "self-realization for all students." Notwithstanding our ongoing criticisms of teaching and schooling, our nation's estimation of the role of teachers as significant agents of society remains relatively constant. Put another way, although each of us may be uneasy about whether teachers conform to our personally held ideals, we do not call for wholesale abandonment of the roles, functions, and responsibilities of teachers in our schools.

Rather than discarding the central notion of "teacher," we reshape, reconceptualize, and "re-form" our views of teachers and teaching. In part, we do this as a consequence of direct experience with schools, our own and our children's. I believe this is particularly true during times of regional or national stress, whether the discomfort is social, cultural, economic, or otherwise. We *depend* on teachers to help us move through the uncertainties of our times and the unpredictable nature of our future. Much of what we want from teachers and for teachers is a reflection of that dependence, that conviction that teachers' work is and will continue to be one of only a few foundations from which we can move toward the possible.

The years that surround the NCCAT early experience have been troubled. Notwithstanding a federal posture similar to "don't worry, by happy," thoughtful observers of the times note declines in economic indicators, an upsurge in crime, a deepening gap between the comfortable and the poverty-stricken, the exponential spread of the modern-day plague of AIDS, a preoccupation of young adults with often ill-gotten material gain, dramatically present illiteracy in children and adults, and an observable diminution of what philosophers have called "the good life" for all. These and other sweeping national issues are the landscape against which NCCAT emerged. They also form the backdrop for rethinking our values about teachers and their work. And, importantly, they become mirrors against which we measure our current ways of providing opportunities for teachers' personal and professional growth and development.

I do not think it is either accidental or coincidental that the idea of the Center came about when it did. Although it is important to acknowledge the creativity, diligence, and persistence of policy makers and educational leaders in North Carolina as they moved the idea into concrete reality, the times implicitly and explicitly *required* that attention be paid to teachers. If it is true that we depend on teachers for much of what we are and what we may become, it is also true that times of stress call for reinvestments in teachers, reiterations of our belief in their importance, and reaffirmations of the national commitment to educational opportunity as provided mainly by teachers.

NCCAT, though, went against the dominant national refrain of how to attend to teachers. Most of the nation, primarily in the forms of state and local policy mandates, became mesmerized by the phantom of scientific certainty in teaching (Good, 1989). This belief in the alleged scientific certainty about "effective" teaching was directed at teachers who were somehow perceived as wanting. The result was a barrage of "reforms"—interventions, assessments, packages, and observable behaviors that these teachers had to adopt and demonstrate. The promises of this attention to ensure "safe" practice by those teachers who were seen as ineffective are yet to be realized. And even if they are realized, usually as student scores on standardized tests, the promises are under increasing fire for their unimaginative nature and their tenuous connection to personal and societal success criteria such as creativity, inventiveness, imagination, efficacy, and problem solving (Lieberman, 1990). NCCAT took a different approach in its investment in rewarding excellent teachers with the opportunity to participate in re-creation rather than respond to externally imposed reform.

NCCAT, then, can be viewed as both a response to and a rejection of the times in which it came to life. It is an expression of the faith of the populace in teachers, while, at the same time, it demonstrates that faith in sharply different ways than most similar expressions around the United States. Rather than concentrate efforts on remedying perceived deficiencies in teachers, individually and collectively, it set out to reward teachers for their excellence in teaching and to reverse some of the long-standing and negative conditions that teachers and others had come to expect as usual. This new and long overdue approach is, to me, characterized by NCCAT's responses to the conditions of teaching, how it carried out those responses through its work, and how the content of the work was conceptualized.

Center Responses to the Conditions of Teaching

NCCAT has been responsive to a number of conditions that make teachers' work lives more difficult than they need to be. Several are discussed here.

Teacher Isolation

In his book, *Among Schoolchildren*, Kidder (1989) writes:

> After spending most of six hours alone with children in one room, a teacher needs to talk to another adult, if only to remind herself that

> she still is an adult. Chris [the teacher in Kidder's book] needed to talk more than most people. She couldn't sort out her thoughts until she had turned them loose into the air. She hated, not solitude, but the silences that cover up emotions. (p. 22)

He might have been talking about all of us who teach or have taught. He also might have substituted "six years" or "two decades" or "a career" for "six hours alone with children."

NCCAT provides teachers with extended opportunities to turn their thoughts loose in safe and supportive contexts. Those thoughts are about matters of importance, issues of social and cultural significance. This "content" or "curriculum" of NCCAT is treated more directly later in this chapter. The point here is that the Center attends directly to one of the unfortunate but pervasive conditions of teaching—the aloneness that surrounds the work of teachers (Sarason, 1971).

This isolation of teachers, one from another and from other adults who might be included as members in an extended intellectually oriented collegial group, has been shown to have a powerful influence on the ways that teachers see themselves, how they think about themselves in the larger society, and how they do or do not alter their practices over years and decades of practice (Griffin, 1986). At one level, perhaps the most profound, is the sense of isolation from ideas and thoughts that might be transformative influences on teaching. In most school situations, teachers are bound by schedules, buildings, "dailiness" that blunt opportunities to connect with new and different visions of teaching and learning. In effect, they have little but their own experiences to guide them to think and act and believe in new and different ways. Many teachers, it is sad to say, accept this condition of isolation not because they are pleased with it but because they believe it to be a necessary feature of their work.

At another level, the isolation of teachers influences how they think of themselves in status or reputational ways (Tikunoff, Ward, & Griffin, 1981). When so-called "feedback" comes primarily or exclusively from students, it is necessarily bounded by students' perceptions, expectations, and personal circumstances. In some situations, students' responses to teachers are invigorating and positive. In others, they are enervating and negative. In either case, though, the responses are limited and probably not helpful as teachers work through the difficult process of seeing themselves as agents of the larger society. Whether or not a student or a group of students "likes" me as a teacher is only one part of the puzzle that, when all the pieces are in place, helps me to locate the real "me."

Teacher isolation, unfortunately, can also be a buttress, a kind of barricade against unpleasant or unwanted news. When this is true, it is unfortunate because it skews teachers' sense of themselves and their practice. It is protective in some ways, but it also can create an unreal state. If I conceive of teaching solely as what I do and what my students and I think about what I do, I am incomplete as a teacher—the meaning I make is necessarily idiosyncratic and unfinished.

NCCAT, it appears, has acknowledged the condition of teacher isolation and has provided opportunities for teachers to become participants in new communities of teachers. These new communities are striking in their attention to multiple opportunities for professional and deeply human interactions. Connections are encouraged, nurtured, and supported. And serious effort goes into ensuring that the new communities of teachers are not temporary but are extended through alumni activities, printed materials, reports of ongoing Center work, and the like.

Teacher Places

Another condition of teaching that seems to have been taken for granted in typical practice is the extraordinarily amenity-free school contexts in which most teachers do their important work. Schools are often unfriendly places, sometimes for children but especially for adults. The "teachers' lounge" is more often than not a converted classroom with discarded furniture and a coffee maker, and is kept in order by a kind of round robin of teacher volunteers. The idea that teachers might benefit from a tastefully designed and carefully maintained gathering place seems not to have occurred to either school building architects or many school faculties and administrators. The impoverished environments for students are decried by many, but the intellectually and aesthetically barren environments for teachers are seldom noted except as another aspect of what teachers have come to accept as their due.

NCCAT takes to heart the impact of the environment on those who inhabit it. Not only are the public spaces pleasing to the eye, but they are stimulating to the intellect, encouraging to the aesthetic self, and supportive of being together as colleagues. This investment in creating a sympathetic environment extends to the ways that teachers are treated at the Center. It is clear to all who visit that the teachers are the *raison d'etre* of NCCAT, not just passersby.

Teaching as an Undifferentiated Occupation

The Center also responds to the prevailing notion that teaching is a "flat" occupation (Little, 1987). For most teachers, even during the early phases of career ladder implementation schemes, there are few differentiations among individuals, except on conventional quantitative terms such as years of service or numbers of advanced degree credits (Griffin, 1985). Seldom, except informally, are some teachers perceived and rewarded as qualitatively different from their peers. It has become the convention that teachers usually do not publicly acknowledge that some may be differentially effective in qualitative ways. The norm is that "a teacher is a teacher is a teacher."

This is understandable from at least two perspectives. First, it is to the benefit of teacher organizations, primarily unions, that members share relatively equally in what can be negotiated in terms of salary, benefits, and the like. It is also convenient for school systems to treat teachers in large subsets of an employee pool, which are determined by verifiable "hard" data such as years in service. Second, views of what constitutes high quality teaching vary, and methods to sort teachers according to the views are, at best, fragile in terms of reliability and validity.

NCCAT, though, has accepted as a fundamental principle that there are "excellent" teachers and that they should be rewarded and supported. The identification of teacher excellence and the subsequent application procedures required of those identified are central concerns of the Center. Testimony to this acknowledgment of excellence in teaching is a major hallmark of the organization and was an early source of support for the idea of the Center.

I am unaware of whether there was any serious questioning of this principle of rewarding excellent teachers. I wonder, though, if there might not be unrealized value in extending NCCAT participation opportunities to teachers more broadly. Is it possible that most teachers, even those not identified by peers and supervisors as outstanding, would find Center seminars rewarding, in the conventional sense, and invigorating? Would teachers in general, rather than teachers as a special subgroup, be sparked to rethink their own status and worth? Would the Center perhaps become a stimulus to excellence as well as a reward for it?

This is not to say that rewarding excellence in teaching is not a desirable and admirable function of NCCAT. It is. But early reports of Center work and its consequences suggest possibilities for most or all teachers. After all, we're not yet certain about what prompts the kind of commitment, dedication, and outcomes that are associated with excellent teachers. Perhaps an NCCAT opportunity or two could be tested as a way to *promote* as well as reward outstanding teaching.

The Importance of Intellectual Connections

Another condition of "teaching as usual" is the distance between most practicing teachers and sources of intellectual stimulation (Griffin, Lieberman, & Jacullo-Noto, 1983). Teaching, even in its most exemplary forms, most often consists of engaging students with the history of a field of study. Although teachers and students, in the best settings, discover and create meaning together, the discoveries are more often than not ones that leaders in the various disciplines have already moved beyond. Teachers, by definition, interact almost exclusively with intellectual and creative novices, not leaders. The effect of this condition of teaching is sometimes the settling into routinized teaching, revisiting the same "discoveries" year after year. Sometimes it does prompt a teacher to take an often lonely journey into familiar and unfamiliar intellectual terrain. But seldom do most teachers together have the opportunity to seek out and engage with experts, whether aesthetic, intellectual, or practical.

NCCAT provides a context in which teachers are connected to leaders in diverse fields. Importantly, the connections are not conventional in that they are rooted in assumptions about how to attend to the "knowledge of most worth," assumptions that move well beyond typical learning situations. Exploration, rather than hearing and remembering, is a central tenet. Interaction around ideas and works of art, rather than responding to others' views, is another. The Center provides the opportunity for teachers to engage the ideas and people at the forefront of ways of knowing and doing, and depends on natural human curiosity and concern for the possible to be accomplished.

Closely related to this sense-making as teachers extend their connections to fields of scholarship and practice is the understanding that these connections, in typical school settings, are most often limited to the school subjects that teachers teach. That is, when school systems make such intellectual connections possible, they are usually restricted to the idea that history teachers connect with history, music teachers with performance artists or composers, and the like. Few opportunities exist for testing the hypothesis that those who are broadly educated and comprehensively sensitive to knowledge and artistry will be more effective teachers of a single school subject. We are typically restrained by the view that our professional growth should be restricted to the content we teach students.

Clearly, NCCAT planners and current staff conceive of learning and discovering and creating as a complex web of human growth, a view very different from those that inform typical practice. Participating teachers cross conventional intellectual boundaries. They discover together the freedom and excitement that come with being a newcomer to knowledge. They are encouraged to invent ways to make meaning outside of their own fields. They experience the possibilities of connections across bodies of knowledge, works of art, and processes of developing social understanding. They come to grips with what Greene (1978) calls becoming "fully engaged." She writes:

> The more fully engaged we are, the more we can look through others' eyes, the more richly individual we become. The activities that compose learning not only engage us in our own quests for answers and for meanings; they also serve to initiate us into the communities of scholarship and . . . into the human community, in its largest and richest sense. (p. 3)

NCCAT has committed its work to promoting this initiation of teachers into broader, more expansive, and, I believe, more rewarding intellectual and social communities.

Obviously, the Center provides participants with a richly intellectual environment, a place where thoughts and thinking are valued, shared, and celebrated. This, unfortunately, is another contrast to prevailing conditions in many of the nation's schools. In the past two decades, there seems to have been a diminution of the idea that expectations for teaching practice are rooted in conceptions of intellectual activity. Instead, we have gone through the "dumbing down" of teaching to a sort of paraprofessionalism. (Elsewhere, I have described these paraprofessional acts of teaching as something that is efficiently mastered, easily observed, and economically remediated [Griffin, 1991].) Instead of conceiving of teaching as requiring deep thought, complex decision making, reflection, analysis, and refinement over time, many policy makers and too many teachers have been convinced that teaching is a variation of painting by the numbers. Packages, panaceas, nostrums, and so on are touted as surefire routes to teaching "effectiveness." Some, unfortunately, have been derived from early faith in the process-product research on teaching. These prescriptions for practice are mounted as staff development programs, used as evaluation criteria for certification, and otherwise misrepresented as scientific certainties (Hoffman et al., 1986).

Teaching, of course, is an extraordinarily complex human activity, depending for success on fully engaging one's intellect with the tasks, the students, and the settings at hand. This engagement is wholeheartedly intellectual.

NCCAT recognizes the importance to teachers and teaching of exercising the intellect. The Center's activities are conceptualized, carried forward, and reflected upon in light of the challenges they present to mind and heart. Those activities free teacher participants to think alone, together, and aloud. They encourage having new ideas, new conceptions, new ways of making sense and drawing relationships between and among disparate bodies of knowledge. They release teachers from the shackles of regimentation, prescription, and set-in-stone standards of practice. Center teachers are, in many senses, liberated to think, not just about their work but also about social, cultural, and intellectual issues that may have been shunted aside in favor of teaching according to others' expectations. NCCAT's commitment to this liberation of the mind is unquestioned and, I think, almost unparalleled.

The attention to teaching as complex, intellectual activity that can be influenced by extending one's grasp of the world of ideas and creative activities outside one's own practical situation is also an expression of the importance of cosmopolitanism, as opposed to provincialism. (Cosmopolitan here does not mean metropolitan. People in cities can be as provincial as those in small-town America. To be cosmopolitan is to have a world view, a wide-ranging set of interests, and a far-reaching distribution of concerns and questions and preoccupations.) Teachers, like other citizens, often become trapped in their own worlds, influenced almost exclusively by their own personal circumstances and dependent on their own experience for guidance. And, as is also true for others, teachers can find themselves trapped inside a provincial world view.

Who in our society should be more cosmopolitan in their perspectives than teachers? Narrow views and limited global perspectives for teachers would match only the belief that teachers should shackle students to the students' present. Broader conceptions of teachers' work—teachers as cosmopolites—match the expectation that students should be well prepared for the unknown; for differences among peoples; in short, for the future. NCCAT provides ample opportunities for teachers to extend their understandings, deepen their sensitivities, explore what is only dimly known or suspected or yearned for.

It isn't just that the NCCAT participants and staff learn for themselves about other places, other media, other ideas, and other worlds. It's that the way they think about and interact around this "otherness" will probably extend their own influence as they work with students. Mary Catherine Bateson (in Moyers, 1989) notes that

> It is possible to look at most problems—whether it is the AIDS epidemic or the conflicts faced by women who work and have children, or the hostage crisis in Iran—and to search for creative solutions. When you do that, you're likely to find that your creative solutions have value outside of the immediate context. They can be transferred or shared or learned from by the society at large. (p. 357)

The Center counteracts, in some cases in topsy turvy ways, a number of other typical conditions of teaching that might also be considered here. Among them are issues of teacher status, time devoted to teachers as thinking human beings, teachers as "workers" in interacting systems where others make significant decisions that affect them, teachers as repositories of requisite knowledge rather than learners, teachers as "invisible" in the larger educational situation, and so on.

What all of this adds up to, of course, is that the Center considers teachers as adults, people who are civilized, self-conscious members of society. Teachers and their work are celebrated at NCCAT in a variety of complex, interacting ways that support the value of teachers and are predicated upon the belief that teachers are concerned with extending their understandings and their influence, and are eager participants in creating their own, and their students', futures.

A Unique Educational Organization

NCCAT is organized to do its work in unconventional ways, ways that sometimes run counter to, or at least are only obliquely like, typical educational organizations. It seems that the Center was purposefully conceptualized as an outlier organization, a model of doing educational work in an intellectually and organizationally sound manner, while maintaining and experimenting with purposeful differences.

The most striking difference to someone who has spent an adult lifetime as an educational professional is the Center's demonstration that organizing for teaching-learning work need not be hierarchical and linear (Schlechty, 1990). It is revealing of the planners' and current staff's way of thinking about the Center to note the "flat" organizational structure, its dependence on horizontal rather than vertical interactions and decision making, its insistence that those persons who know (rather than those who are presumed by position to know) be involved in planning and doing, and its flexibility in promoting this ease of authority position.

It might be argued that NCCAT is such a special institution with such a special status conceptualization that such a rearrangement of business as usual could be expected. A few moments reflection, however, denies this view as having any predictive power. Think of the "new" organizational entities that have dotted the educational history of the past several decades. Most, I believe, either have never been considered in the organizational terms NCCAT seems to manifest or have reverted quickly to bureaucracies that mirror the conventional labor-management, status and power distribution educational settings that are so common to our shared understanding. Yet, experts on organizational health and productivity are more directly aligned with the ways NCCAT does its work. Peters (1987), for one, urges leaders to move from the "hierarchical" to "flat" organizations with "barriers broken" between roles (p. 53).

Although it may not have been purposefully done, the Center seems to be a counterpoint to the widespread conventions of masculine ways of knowing and doing. Indeed, it seems to mirror what some believe to be the ways that women think, work, and create and support relationships. Rather than being highly compartmentalized, NCCAT is intricately interdependent in its organization. Rather than having well-defined roles and responsibilities, the staff works fluidly across organizational boundaries. Rather than having rigid work schedules, people shift in and out of work expectations and requirements, always seeing that the work is done, of course. Instead of one-way communication systems, the talk and writing are multidirectional. Instead of separate "departments" of activity, there is an obvious set of intricate intellectual and practical connections throughout the Center.

Another striking difference between NCCAT and typical educational settings is the serious and ongoing attention paid to the importance of accompanying the work with opportunities to reflect upon and analyze what is going on. Usually, education-focused organizations, particularly elementary and secondary schools, are caught up almost exclusively with the "dailiness" of what is done. Schools are organized to capture students for sustained periods of time, time that educators usually think must be occupied with conventional learning tasks and supervised by teachers. This dominant theme of schools as organizations allows few opportunities for thinking alone or collectively about how or even whether educational work is accomplished and made meaningful for those concerned.

NCCAT, on the other hand, appears to have a core belief that its work must not become routinized, must be re-made even when situations, as in the case of repeated seminars, are similar. On the one hand, it could be argued that this is only natural in light of NCCAT's other dissimilarities from typical educational institutions. Yet, what other innovative educational situations have adopted and sustained this stance? Wouldn't it have been possible, perhaps even probable, that NCCAT would have set itself up as a conventional school-like place for teachers to learn more? Mightn't seminars have been planned as lockstep engagements with knowledge? Isn't it conceivable that teacher participants might have been scheduled and slotted and otherwise fitted into a tight, nonreflective routine? And, importantly, mightn't that have been an easier, more accustomed route to follow than one that rests on reflection, flexibility, redirection, and adaptation?

NCCAT, in obvious and subtle ways, demonstrates a sensitivity toward and a consideration of its clients, the participants in its activities. Clearly, a series of decisions have been made that focus directly on who the Center is for—these participants. Although this seems to be an obvious focus, think of the number of organizations in our society that seem not to understand that their work is for the benefit of clients rather than employees, organizational leaders, and/or patrons.

The Center's wholehearted attention to the teachers, and others who visit for seminars, reunions, and other activities, is seen in a variety of ways, not just in the provision of thoughtful amenities, as already noted. Much of the content of the seminars derives from teachers' interests and curiosities, sometimes in terms of initial offerings and often in the ways that seminars are revised and redirected on the spot. Apparently, it is not unusual for teachers' suggestions for changes in topic, time, or focus to be acted upon by Center staff and seminar leaders. Of course, this practice is one of the centerpieces of good teaching, but it is seldom encountered outside excellently run elementary and secondary classrooms. In particular, school system-level professional development opportunities for teachers are seldom sensitive to teachers' expectations and self-expressed needs. Rather, they are most often developed according to school officials' *perceptions* of teachers' needs. This is a big difference.

Another organizational feature of the Center that deserves attention is the persistent use of philosophical and other humanist perspectives as the reasons for specific actions. In contrast to the hyperscientism that seems to pervade educational organizations currently, NCCAT bases its decisions firmly on beliefs, assumptions, and values. The quasi-scientific is not ignored, of course, but the forms of planning and implementation discourse at NCCAT appear to be based firmly on belief systems. This is most dramatic in relation to the seminar offerings (see below), which conform not to somehow better preparing teachers to give specific instruction to students but to expanding and extending teachers' opportunities to become wholehearted participants in intellectual, societal, and cultural arenas much more far-reaching than those of classrooms and schools.

Several beliefs about teachers appear to me to pervade the work of the Center. My outsider's view would include these:

- Teachers are curious, intellectually able, and inventive.
- At the heart of teaching is the teacher's skill in and willingness to transcend conventional school subject boundaries.
- Teachers can and should be partners in determining their own learning.
- Teachers are professionals who have sufficient knowledge, skill, and experience in common to promote important collegial learning.
- Teachers' expectations for intellectual and creative opportunities to learn are consistently high.
- Teachers' interests are broadly comprehensive and "connect" with their teaching, even when they appear to be distinct from the content of their teaching.
- Teachers make these connections as a matter of course, not because they are stimulated by outsiders to do so.

I am not certain if my interpretation of how Center planners and current staff members think of doing their work is shared by these people. I *am* certain that these beliefs can be tracked through NCCAT's activities, its initial formulation, and its current operational procedures.

Although I know that the Center tracks numbers of participants, amount of time spent, and other quantitative ways of demonstrating what it does, I am struck by the apparent belief at NCCAT that "telling the story" in words, rather than as a compilation of numerical tables and such, is the appropriate representation of its work. The attention to myths, the importance of rituals, the concern for developing and attending to discourse systems, and the investment in cultural and other humanities-oriented events all provide a picture of NCCAT as an evolving story, maybe even a set of "tales told," through which runs strands of intellectuality, social responsibility, and cultural sensitivity.

The "Curriculum" of the Center

It is important to comment, even briefly, on the content of the Center's work, partly because of its dramatic difference from other opportunities teachers have to grow and develop as professionals and partly because of its own integrity, independent of comparisons with conventional staff development programs for teachers. Some of the other content of this chapter has touched on these matters, but certain points seem important to make here.

First, NCCAT seems to have gripped the issue of intellectual provincialism by the throat and wrestled it to the ground. The content of Center activities is consistently sophisticated, broadly comprehensive, integrated across disciplines, and focused on a visionary perspective of what teacher learning can be. This is sharply different from much staff development content that zeroes in on fragments of teaching and treats those fragments as though they were isolated from the rich and complex worlds that teachers and students inhabit together (Howey & Vaughan, 1983).

Second, the Center acknowledges and acts upon the notion that the aesthetic dimensions of our shared world are important elements of being human. There are conscious and deliberate choices about what will be presented to teachers that incorporate the arts, both as artifacts of the Center context and objects of attention for seminars.

Third, there is a clear picture of the Center as a context for learning that rests upon an understanding of the power of multisensory experiences in teaching and learning. It is common—probably expected by Center staff—for activities to attend to a carefully thought out combination of talk, reading, questioning, engagement with performing arts, taste, smell, touch, sentiment, intellectuality, creativity, and other ways of knowing. I haven't heard or read the old saw that "if one stimulus doesn't work, we'll try another" in connection with NCCAT. Instead, I infer from what I know of the Center that this "either-or" proposition is replaced by a comprehensive view of people as multiply talented and, consequently, more positively engaged with learning opportunities that call upon this array of possibilities.

Fourth, it seems that the Center depends to an extent on "verified" knowledge for its content, but uses that knowledge as a base from which participants are urged, encouraged, supported, and otherwise connected with opportunities to construct their own meaning, create their own perspectives, and draw their own conclusions. This perspective, of course, fits nicely with other features of the Center, particularly the perceived beliefs about teacher clients mentioned above. It is obviously a perspective that is in major ideological and practical conflict with conventional and widespread ideas about how to "reform" teaching and schools by injecting them with what others have come to believe to be so.

Fifth, the content of the Center appears to be selected *because* it is amenable to group exploration, invention, and "making meaning together." Interestingly, in most school-like situations, groups of children (and adults) are brought together for instruction, but the learning is expected to be private, isolated, and individual. The group structure is more a way to ensure efficiency and economy than it is to promote, encourage, and reward people for learning with and from one another. NCCAT seems to turn this typical pattern around in its deliberate planning for how seminar participants can influence one another and enrich the encounters with seminar curricula.

Last, and perhaps the most important aspect of the content of the Center to me, is the acknowledgment that being a teacher in today's society has profound ethical and moral dimensions. It is clear to this outsider that the Center's curriculum is rooted in a deep and abiding faith in the importance of exploration into what is right and wrong, good and bad, true and false. This isn't indoctrination or "truth telling" or some other form of asserting a viewpoint. Instead, the Center's curriculum demonstrates topic selections that *must* cause participants to grapple alone and together with ethical issues, moral perspectives, and the consequences of choices among them. Few other educational settings that teachers encounter offer this engagement with the complexities of living and learning in our society. If this were the only comment I could make about the Center, it would be sufficient to answer the question, "Can we learn from NCCAT?" with a resounding, "Yes!"

Conclusion

The outsider's view presented here is an expression of enthusiasm for NCCAT and what it has accomplished. This enthusiasm, of course, is not objective; it doesn't stem from a dispassionate disinterest in teacher renewal. Instead, this interpretation of what NCCAT means in the larger arena of educational reform is constructed from bits and pieces of views of teaching as intellectual activity, teachers as thinking and caring professionals, and educational situations as central social and cultural artifacts of our shared experience.

I am encouraged by NCCAT in a variety of ways. The high value placed on teachers is a belief I share. The conception of teachers as thoughtful members of an extended collegium makes sense to me. Reconsidering teacher reform from remediation to reward rings true, especially because it follows a decade of what I believe is the trivialization of teaching activity. And, policy-level investments in these and other conceptually similar efforts are examples of enlightened policy decisions seldom encountered in what I consider the overregulated world of schools.

My personal and professional belief is that NCCAT can continue to be a source of information and enlightenment about teacher renewal. This will happen in large measure in direct relation to the willingness of Center staff and teacher participants to continue to systematically think aloud in public about their work. This book is a first step toward that end.

References

Carnegie Forum on Education and the Economy. (1986). *A nation prepared: Teachers for the 21st century.* Washington, DC: Author.

Good, T. (1989, January). *Using classroom and school research to professionalize teaching.* Paper presented at the International Congress for Effective Schooling, Rotterdam, The Netherlands.

Greene, M. (1978). *Landscapes of learning.* New York: Teachers College Press.

Griffin, G. (1985). The school as a workplace and the master teacher concept. *Elementary School Journal, 86*(1), 1-16.

Griffin, G. (1986). Thinking about teaching. In K. Zumwalt (Ed.), *Improving teaching* (1986 Yearbook of the Association for Supervision and Curriculum Development) (pp. 101-113). Washington, DC: ASCD.

Griffin, G. (1990). The future of teachers and teaching: Imperatives and possibilities. *Peabody Journal of Education, 65*(3), 74-87.

Griffin, G. (1991). Teacher education and curriculum decision making: The issue of teacher professionalism. In F. Klein (Ed.), *The politics of curriculum decision making* (pp. 121-150). Albany: State University of New York Press.

Griffin, G., Lieberman, A., & Jacullo-Noto, J. (1983). *Interactive research and development on schooling: Final report.* New York: Teachers College, Columbia University.

Hoffman, J., Edwards, S., Barnes, S., Griffin, G., Paulissen, M., & O'Neal, S. (1986). *Clinical teacher education guidelines*. Austin, TX: Research and Development Center for Teacher Education.

The Holmes Group. (1986). *Tomorrow's teachers*. East Lansing, MI: Author.

Howey, K., & Vaughan, J. (1983). Current patterns of staff development. In G. Griffin (Ed.), *Staff development* (Eighty-second Yearbook of the National Society for the Study of Education) (pp. 92-117). Chicago: University of Chicago Press.

Kidder, T. (1989). *Among schoolchildren*. Boston: Houghton Mifflin.

Lieberman, A. (Ed.). (1990). *Schools as collaborative cultures: Creating the future now*. New York: Falmer Press.

Little, J. (1987). Teachers as colleagues. In V. Richardson-Koehler (Ed.), *Educator's handbook: A research perspective* (pp. 491-518). New York: Longman.

Moyers, B. (1989). *A world of ideas*. New York: Doubleday.

Peters, T. (1987). *Thriving on chaos*. New York: Harper & Row.

Sarason, S. (1971). *The culture of the school and the problem of change*. New York: Allyn & Bacon.

Schlechty, P. (1990). *Schools for the 21st century*. San Francisco: Jossey-Bass.

Tikunoff, W., Ward, B., & Griffin, G. (1981). Interactive research and development as a form of professional growth. In K. Howey, R. Bents, & D. Corrigan (Eds.), *School-focused inservice: Descriptions and discussions* (pp. 187-215). Reston, VA: The Association of Teacher Educators.

Chapter 8

Charting the Course: The Center's Future Role in Teacher Renewal

WALTER P. OLDENDORF and ANTHONY G. RUD JR.

Up to now, NCCAT has occupied a special niche in the world of teacher education. Unlike inservice workshops, the Center deliberately avoids directly addressing the concerns of the classroom in either teaching content or strategy. Unlike graduate programs in education, NCCAT does not require exams or papers, nor does it give grades or credit. The Center does not make any claims for a causal connection between its programs and higher level of student achievement in the classrooms of its alumni.

The Center, therefore, does not appear to duplicate or compete with other programs of teacher development. This status is no doubt in large part responsible for the relatively benign attitude toward NCCAT on the part of other professionals and organizations involved in teacher development. One wonders, though, if this will change as Center programs expand to include more than 1,000 teachers each year. As the Center and other similar programs become more visible in teacher development, increasing demands will be heard for adequate rationales for their role.

Indeed, continuing expansion of Center programs inevitably raises the question posed by Griffin in Chapter 7, who asks whether:

> There might not be unrealized value in extending NCCAT participation opportunities to teachers more broadly. Is it possible that most teachers, even those not identified by peers and supervisors as outstanding, would find Center seminars rewarding, in the conventional sense, and invigorating?

That happy conclusion would seem, of course, much to be desired. A less sanguine possibility would be that the continuing expansion of the Center's clientele would begin to include a population whose *developmental* needs were less congruent with current Center offerings.

We emphasize possible developmental differences in needs, rather than asserting that *excellent* teachers will profit from Center offerings, and *less than excellent* teachers may or may not profit. This developmental concept suggests that teachers move through qualitatively different states of thinking about the nature of teaching and their own concerns about being a good teacher, and that their needs change accordingly.

Indeed, researchers (Borich, 1988, pp. 62-72) have observed three such stages of development characterized successively by self-concerns, instructional concerns, and student concerns. Clearly, a Center program might well be perceived as less relevant by a teacher at the stage of self-concern, and more relevant by a teacher at the stage of student concerns. At the third stage, a teacher is thinking about the values inherent in the context of learning. NCCAT experiences may therefore become appropriate for most teachers at some point in their careers and inappropriate at other points. Whether this is true is an empirical question that the Center should be addressing. NCCAT will need to think more carefully about its fit on the continuum of teacher development as its programs encompass larger segments of the teaching population.

Perhaps the most significant contribution of NCCAT to teacher development may be related to Goodlad's eighth postulate set forth in *Teachers for Our Nation's Schools* (1990). Goodlad urges

> Programs for the education of educators must provide extensive opportunities for future teachers to move beyond being students of organized knowledge to become teachers who inquire into both knowledge and its teaching. . . . What is called for is . . . an inquiry into the means for teaching embedded in the domains of knowledge. (p. 58)

Goodlad goes on to suggest that transcending the schism between pedagogy and subject-matter knowledge should begin early as part of the student's general education during the preservice years. Though NCCAT does not offer preservice teacher education, its programs epitomize the process that Goodlad recommends. As we saw in the seminar narrative in Chapter 4, the most powerful metaphors from the disciplines merge with the most effective pedagogy to provide a model for teaching and learning. The schism between the disciplines and pedagogy disappears in this context.

The loss of status, respect, and freedom by our nation's teachers is a sad part of American education. Our efforts in this book have been to speak of ways that the conditions of teachers can be addressed and made better for all concerned. Both Seymour Sarason and North Carolina teacher Jean Powell speak of the need for teachers (indeed perhaps all adults) to have opportunities for continual learning.

> The assumption that teachers can create and maintain those conditions which make school learning and school living stimulating for [the young] without those same conditions existing for teachers, has no warrant in the history of man. . . . Dewey knew all this well. . . . [He] created the conditions for his teachers which he wanted them to create for their students. (Sarason, 1972, pp. 123-24; see also Sarason, 1990, Chapter 8)

> We have a governor's school for students. Why not the same for teachers? (Powell, 1983)

We have proposed, by means of this study of a teacher renewal effort, a concrete and in some instances practical companion piece to earlier, more speculative work by others (Bolin & Falk, 1987). The importance of re-creating oneself through a continuous adventure for the intellect, in company with others of like mind in a supportive haven, is a theme that runs throughout this book.

Such a task is not easy. In Figure 8.1, the director of the North Carolina Arboretum, George Briggs, alerts us to concerns for his and all organizations. Dreams or visions of the future must be enacted for the health and growth of organizations and individuals. What might be part of such a vision?

We might begin with a fresh metaphor for schools, or at least one not yet eroded and depleted of meaning. Such metaphors have in the past been uninspiring to educators. Schools as factories or as battlefields are familiar and tired images.

On ancient Cherokee land, the state of North Carolina has erected three new buildings for its teachers. Fittingly, they have been given Cherokee names: Katusi, Atanto, and Ahysti. Together these words mean "a place in the mountains for the exploration of the human spirit." These words convey a sense of learning in comfort, of hospitality writ large in an educational setting, and perhaps even of schools as safe havens for their inhabitants. Not an easy task, given the almost intractable problems of our public schools that we and others encounter almost daily in our outreach work in impoverished communities. Yes, a vision is no replacement for hard work in the trenches.

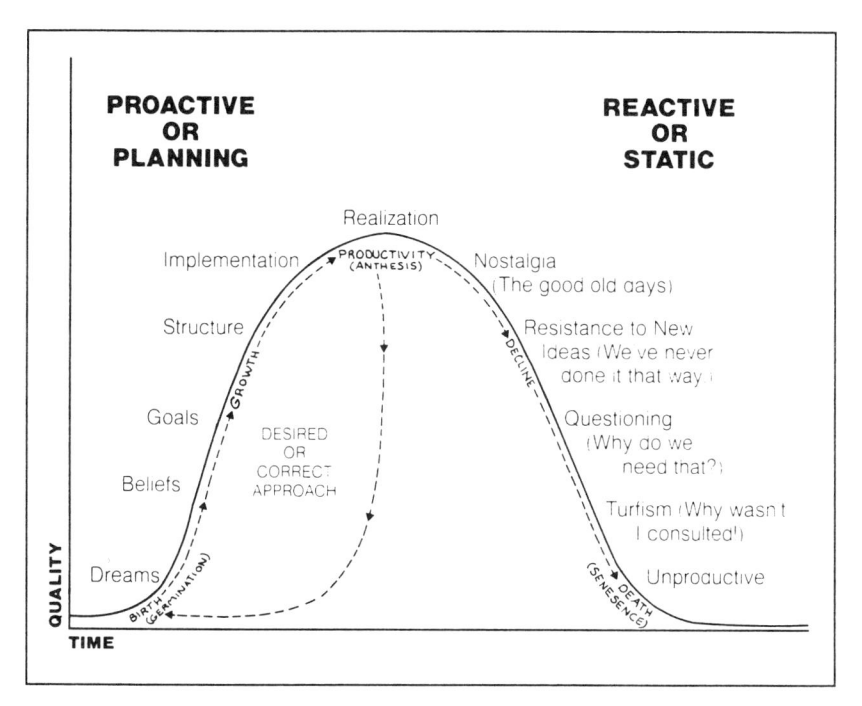

Figure 8.1: Life Cycle of an Institution.

```
PROACTIVE                              REACTIVE
OR                                     OR
PLANNING                               STATIC

                    Realization
       Implementation  PRODUCTIVITY   Nostalgia
                       (ANTHESIS)     (The good old days)
       Structure                      Resistance to New
                                      Ideas (We've never
                                      done it that way.)
       Goals        DESIRED           Questioning
                    OR                (Why do we
                    CORRECT           need that?)
       Beliefs      APPROACH
                                      Turfism (Why wasn't
                                      I consulted!)
       Dreams                         Unproductive
QUALITY
 BIRTH                                 DEATH
 (GERMINATION)                         (SENESCENCE)
TIME
```

Healthy organizations fall within the dream building cycle on the proactive side of the curve, choosing with each dream realization to spawn a new dream.

From Dream a little before you pick up that shovel, by G. Briggs, and W. McDevitt, 1989, *The Public Garden* 4(1), p. 16. Reprinted by permission.

Let us keep the vision, though, and turn to what can be done. In Chapter 3, we saw that the realization that teaching itself, with its attendant inquiry and wonder, can be renewing. This realization transformed a job into a calling for Vivian Paley. Other efforts also stress these generative aspects of teaching (Bolin & Falk, 1987; Duckworth, 1987; Haroutunian-Gordon, 1991).

We can hear the gentle reminder of a teacher as we sketch these thoughts for the future.

> I know why I got into teaching. I am *not* burned out, despite what the media say! Just give me support, the time to grow and

develop my mind, and *listen* to me and respect what I have to say. Leave me to do the teaching!

Places like NCCAT, and initiatives by others elsewhere, can assist in the care and support of teachers in such adventures for the intellect. It may be a small, but not unimportant, effort.

References

Bolin, F., & Falk, J. (1987). *Teacher renewal: Professional issues, personal choices*. New York: Teachers College Press.

Borich, G. (1988). *Effective teaching methods*. Columbus, OH: Merrill.

Duckworth, E. (1987). *"The having of wonderful ideas" and other essays on teaching and learning*. New York: Teachers College Press.

Goodlad, J. (1990). *Teachers for our nation's schools*. San Francisco: Jossey-Bass.

Haroutunian-Gordon, S. (1991). *Turning the soul: Teaching through conversation in the high school*. Chicago: University of Chicago Press.

Powell, J. P (1983, November 29). Speech to the North Carolina Commission on Education for Economic Growth.

Sarason, S. (1972). *The creation of settings and the future societies*. San Francisco: Jossey-Bass.

Sarason, S. (1990). *The predictable failure of educational reform: Can we change course before it's too late?*. San Francisco: Jossey-Bass.

About the Editors and Contributors

William E. Bickel is a senior scientist at the Learning Research and Development Center (LRDC) and associate professor of education at the University of Pittsburgh. He was educated at Oberlin College, and received his master's and doctoral degrees in education from the University of Pittsburgh. Prior to coming to the university, Bickel was a public school teacher and administrator. His research interests include educational evaluation research, educational policy related to at-risk youth, and the professional development of teachers. Bickel is the coauthor, with William W. Cooley, of *Decision-Oriented Educational Research* (Kluwer).

William W. Cooley is the director of the Pennsylvania Educational Policy Studies at LRDC and professor of education at the University of Pittsburgh. He was educated at Lawrence College and received his doctoral degree in education from Harvard University. His research interests are focused on educational planning, policy, and evaluation studies. He also directs a doctoral program with that title in the school of education. He has coauthored four books with P. R. Lohnes and one with William E. Bickel, *Decision-Oriented Educational Research* (Kluwer).

Maxine Greene is William F. Russell Professor Emeritus in the Foundations of Education at Teachers College, Columbia University. She received her doctoral degree from New York University. Greene is past president of the American Educational Research Association, American Educational Studies Association, and Philosophy of Education Society. She has published over 70 articles, numerous chapters in books, and several books, including most recently *The Dialectic of Freedom* (Teachers College Press). Greene served as editor of *Teachers College Record* from 1965-1970. In 1984, she was elected to the National Academy of Education.

Gary A. Griffin is professor of education at the University of Arizona. Prior to that position, Griffin was dean of the college of education at the University of Illinois at Chicago, He received his bachelor's, master's, and doctoral degrees from UCLA. His scholarly interests include teacher education, the professional development of experienced teachers, school improvement, and curricular change. Recent publications include "Curriculum Decision Making for Teacher Education" in *Theory into Practice*, "The Future of Teachers and Teaching" in the *Peabody Journal of Education*, and "Teacher Education and Curriculum Decision Making" in *The Politics of Curriculum Decision Making: Issues in Legislating and Centralizing Curriculum*, edited by Frances Klein (SUNY Press). Griffin has also written the section on teacher education to be included in the forthcoming *Encyclopedia of Educational Research*, 6th Ed., edited by Marvin Alkin (Macmillan).

Diane K. Hoffbauer is an assistant professor of education at Mankato (Minnesota) State University. She received her bachelor's degree there, her master's degree at SUNY-Oneonta, and her doctorate in education at the University of South Carolina. Her dissertation under Craig Kridel focused on the early history of NCCAT. She has taught in Sweden, at a refugee camp in Thailand, and with teachers in Jamaica.

R. Bruce McPherson became the first full-time director of NCCAT in 1986, and served until 1991. He is presently visiting professor for outreach programs at the University of Illinois at Chicago. He received his bachelor's and master's degrees from the University of Rochester, and his Ph.D. in educational administration from the University of Chicago. He has been a junior and senior high school English teacher, principal, associate superintendent, superintendent, independent school head, and, prior to coming to NCCAT, professor of education at the University of Illinois at Chicago. McPherson has published widely in the fields of educational administration and policy. He is the coauthor of *Managing Uncertainty* (Merrill).

Walter P. Oldendorf (editor) is associate dean of the college and chair of programs in education at Western Montana College of the University of Montana. He served as interim associate director for programming at NCCAT from 1987 to 1990. Oldendorf received his bachelor's degree from Stanford University, and his master's and Ph.D. in social studies education from Northwestern University. He taught for 12 years in the middle grades of the Illinois public schools and at the laboratory school of Illinois State University. He has also taught at National-Louis University and was associate professor of education at Berea College prior to coming to NCCAT. His professional interests include phenomenological and Deweyan approaches to teacher education.

Anthony G. Rud Jr. (editor) is a senior fellow at NCCAT. He received his bachelor's degree from Dartmouth College, and his master's and Ph.D. in philosophy from Northwestern University. He has taught high school social studies and humanities, worked as a college administrator and faculty member, served on committees of the American Educational Research Association and American Philosophical Association, and is consulted widely on critical thinking and philosophy for children. His current scholarly activities include working with teachers around the country as a senior associate of the Council for Basic Education, evaluating a program in moral education for Boston University, and coediting a forthcoming volume of essays with James W. Garrison on concepts missing from current educational discourse.

Christine M. Shea is a senior fellow at NCCAT. She received her Ph.D. in educational policy studies, specializing in the history of education, at the University of Illinois at Urbana-Champaign. She has taught at the University of Illinois, Hampshire College, and West Virginia University. She serves on the editorial board of *Educational Theory* and is a member of the executive committee of the American Educational Studies Association. Her recently coedited book, *The New Servants of Power,* won *Choice* magazine's "Outstanding Academic Book, 1989" award. She is currently completing a book dealing with an analysis of contemporary models of adult education.

Index

Accountability, 88
Action for Excellence: A Comprehensive Plan to Improve Our Nation's Schools, 27
Adler, M., 19, 45
Administration. *See* Educational leadership
Adopt-a-School Program, 26
Aesthetic experience, 20-22, 142
  importance of, 54-56
  in practice, 58-59
Alumni reunions, 84-85, 105-106
Among Schoolchildren (Kidder), 131-132
Appalachian Regional Commission (ARC), 30-32
Architecture, landscape, 58-59, 81
Arcilla, R., 49
Art, 81
Artistic experience. *See* Aesthetic experience
Ashton, P. T., 10
Aspen Institute, 33, 36
Authority
  delegation of, 95-98
  nature of, 94-95

Bacon, F., 16
Barnard, C. I., 87
Barnard, H., 4
Bateson, M. C., 138
Bickel, W. E., *xii*, 37, 40-41, 112-127
Bishop, L., 102-103
Blatz, W., 9
Bloom, B., 47
Bolin, F., *xi*, 2, 148, 149
Borich, G., 147
Boyce, A. C., 7
Briggs, G., 148, 149
Brooks, T., 59

Brown, L., 49
Bruner, J., 54
Buchmann, M., 49
Bunzel, J., 6
Burgess, E. W., 9
Burke, P. J., 2
Burns, J. M., 60
Business and economics, 81
Byer, K. S., 80

Caring relationship, 59-60
Cary, F., 27
Cedoline, A., 10
Center. *See* North Carolina Center for the Advancement of Teaching (NCCAT)
Center for the Advancement and Renewal of Educators (CARE), San Francisco, 70
Challenge to American Schools (Grant), 6
Chambers, G., 34, 42
Charters, W. W., 8
Civil rights movement, 80
Classless Profession: American Schoolmen in the Nineteenth Century (Mattingly), 4
Collegiality, 106
  importance of, 121
  nature of, 89, 90
  at NCCAT, 90-94
  organizational structure and, 88, 93-94, 139
Commitment, 90, 103-107
  flow between individual and institution, 104-106
  incentive system and, 106
Commonwealth Fund, 8
Commonwealth Teacher Training Study, The (Charters and Waples), 8

155

Community of inquiry, 50-51
Community Schools Program, 26
Competency-based teacher education, 8
Competency Testing Program, 26
Cooley, C. H., 9, 10
Cooley, W. W., *xii*, 37, 40, 41, 112-127
Cornell, J., 82
Cosmopolitanism, 137
Crowson, R. L., 12, 98, 104
Cuban, L., 2
Cultural socialization, 3, 9-10, 64-65
Curriculum, *xii*, 63-86, 142-143
  aesthetic approach in, 58-59, 142
  alumni reunions, 84-85, 105-106
  cultural transmission in, 64-65
  evaluation of seminars and, 77-79, 114-117, 125-126
  features of NCCAT program, 68-69
  global alumni seminars, 85-86
  "Humans on Earth" seminar, 68-79
  isolation of teachers and, 131-133
  special interest program, 84
  standard seminars, 68-83, 91, 102, 114-117, 125-126
  student-centered approach, 65
  teacher scholar program, 83-84
Curriculum praxis, 1
Czikszentmihalyi, M., 98

Dance, 55
Darling-Hammond, L., 45, 121
Davis, C., 82
Decision-making
  moral, 18-20
  social, 9
Decision-oriented educational research, elements of, 113
Dellinger, D., 57
Denton, V., 38
Devaney, R., 83
Dewey, J., *viii*, 9, 14, 45, 55, 64, 99
Dickson, G. E., 2
Disciplinary imperialism, 11
Duckworth, E., 49, 52-53, 149
duPont, P., 27
Dykeman, W., 80

Economics and business, 81
Edgerton, C., 80

Educational leadership, *xii*, 87-111
  accountability and, 88
  caring relationship and, 59-60
  collegiality and, 89-94, 106, 121
  commitment and, 90, 103-107
  efficacy and, 87-88
  flexibility and, 88
  learning organization and, 90, 98-103
  modeling and, 88
  moral responsibility and, 90, 94-98
  structure of organization, 88, 93-94, 139
Educational reform, 120-122
  cultural, 3, 8-10
  current pressures in, 129-131
  metaphor of cultural transmission in, 63-68
  moral, 3, 4-7
  of the 1980s, 3, 8, 26-27, 45
  renewal as basis of, 59-60
  student-centered approach, 8-10, 65
  teacher renewal vs., *xi*
Education Commission of the States, 27
Education for Economic Growth: An Action Plan for North Carolina, 29-30
Effective teaching, 131, 136
Efficacy, 87-88
Efficiency movement, 7-8
Environmental studies, 81-82
Etzioni, A., 104
Evaluation, formative, 40-41, 87, 112, 113-119
  agenda definition in, 113-117
  purpose of, 112
  reporting in, 115-117
  of seminars by teachers, 77-79, 114-117
  teacher characteristics, 121
  transferring of, to NCCAT, 118-119
Evaluation, summative, 87, 112, 119-126
  educational reform and NCCAT, 120-122
  follow-up study of participants, 122-125
  purpose of, 112-113
  question development in, 119-120
  teacher commentary and, 125-126
  teacher participation in NCCAT, 122
  teacher renewal and NCCAT, 120-122
  timing of, 112-113
Excellent teachers, 8, 147

Facilities development, 33
Falk, J., *xi*, 2, 148, 149
Federal Office of Education, 9-10
Few Thoughts on the Powers and Duties of Women, A (Mann), 5
Flexibility, 88
Formative evaluation. *See* Evaluation, formative
Freedom
  of aesthetic experience, 55
  hospitality and, 56-57
  knowledge and, 46-47, 55, 137
Friday, W., 31, 38, 39
Functions of the Executive (Barnard), 87

Gardiner, P., 55
Getzels, J. W., 98, 103-104
Gibson, M. E., 80
Gifford, J., 37
Gilligan, C., 49
Giovinco, J., 70
Glass, B., 36
Global alumni seminars, 85-86
Goethe, J., 55
Good, T., 131
Goodlad, J., 147
Governor's School, 26
Grant, G., 6
Greene, M., 136
Greer, P., 48
Griffin, G. A., *xii*, 56, 128-145, 146

Habermas, J., 12
Hanna, C., 95-97
Hardy, S., 96
Haroutunian-Gordon, S., 149
Harvey, C., 70-71, 73, 74
Hillenbrand, M., 37
Hoffbauer, D. K., *xii*, 25-44, 46
Hoffman, J., 137
Hopkins, M., 28
Hospitality, 133
  ethos of, 56-57
  in practice, 58-59
Howey, K., 142
Huebner, D., 63, 66-68, 83
Hughes, L., 72, 74
"Humans on Earth" seminar, 68-79

Hunt, J. B., Jr., 23
  Education Commission of the States and, 27
  education initiatives in North Carolina and, 26-27
  formation of NCCAT and, 30-42
  North Carolina Commission on Education for Economic Growth, 25, 27-30, 108

Incentive systems, 106
Ingwerson, D., 59
Interdisciplinary teaching and learning, 49
International programming, 82
Isolation, of teachers, 131-133

Jackson, R., 30
Jacullo-Noto, J., 135
Jolley, H., 74
Jones, S., 79

Kanter, R. M., 104
Kennedy, M. M., 17
Kidder, T., 131-132
Knowledge
  as base for further learning, 142-143
  cultural transmission approach, 64-65
  freedom and, 46-47, 55, 137
  nature of, 48-49, 67-68
  pedagogical content, 46-47
  self-, 53-54
Kohlberg, L., 63-65
Kolb, D. A., 98

Landscape architecture, 58-59, 81
Leadership. *See* Educational leadership
Learning
  knowledge as base for, 142-143
  peak experiences in, 47-48
  by teachers, 45, 51-52, 64-68
Learning organization, 90, 98-103
  abstract conceptualization and, 98, 101
  active experimentation and, 98, 99, 101-102
  concrete experience and, 98, 99-100
  reflective observation and, 98, 100-101
Leland, E., 32
Levine, M., 36
Lieberman, A., 129, 131, 135

Lipman, M., 50
List, D., 36
Literature, 80
Little, J., 134
Logical analysis, 17
Lorenz, E., 83

McCarter, D., 69, 75-76
MacCready, P., 37
McDevitt, W., 149
McKinney, M., 34-36, 40
McNutt F., 37
McPherson, R. B., *xii*, 1, 2-3, 12, 13, 54, 57, 60, 70, 87-111
Magill, S., 36
Mann, H., 5-6
Martin, G., 36, 37
Martin, J., 32
Mathematics, 26, 82-83
Mattingly, P., 4
Mayer, R., 63-65
Mead, G. H., 9
Melder, K., 5
Melville, H., *viii*
Methods for Measuring Teachers' Efficiency (Boyce), 7
Miles, R. E., 104
Miller, J. W., 80
Milner, E., 57, 109-110
Moby Dick (Melville), *viii*
Modeling, 88
Moral decision making, 18-20
Moral education, 48-49
Moral reform movement, 3, 4-7
Moral responsibility
 delegation of, 95-98, 106
 nature of, 90, 94-95
Moyers, B., 138
Multisensory experience, 15-16, 142
Music, 80-81

Nash, P., 8
National Teacher Examination (NTE), 121
Nation at Risk: The Imperative for Educational Reform, 26-27
NCCAT. *See* North Carolina Center for the Advancement of Teaching
Noddings, N., 49, 60
North Carolina Association of Educators (NCAE), 30, 35

North Carolina Association of School Administrators, 30
North Carolina Center for the Advancement of Teaching (NCCAT), *xi*
 administration of. *See* Educational leadership
 conditions of teaching and, 131-138
 criteria for teacher renewal
 philosophy, 12-15
 curriculum of. *See* Curriculum
 evaluation and. *See* Evaluation, formative; Evaluation, summative
 facilities development, 33
 feminine approach to learning and, 139
 future of, 146-150
 genesis of idea for, 25-30
 governance and appropriation, 37-40
 institutionalization of programs, 41-42
 mission, conception of, 30-37
 organizational structure of, 88, 93-94, 139
 Planning Committee, 31-37, 40-42
 programming decisions, 34-35, 40-41
 rationale for teacher renewal and, 46-54
 as response to educational environment, 129-131
 screening of teachers for, 47, 100-101, 122, 134-135
 sensory experience and, 15-16, 142
 summer pilot programs, 35-37, 41, 79-80, 115
 teacher renewal as aesthetic praxis, 20-22
 teacher renewal as moral decision making, 18-20
 teacher renewal as skills development, 16-17
 teacher renewal as sociocultural expression, 18
 uniqueness of, 138-142
North Carolina Commission on Education for Economic Growth (NCCEEG), 25, 27-30, 108
North Carolina Scholars program, 26
North Carolina School of Science and Mathematics, 26
North Carolina Writing Project, 26
Nouwen, H., 56-57

Obermiller, T., 54
Oglesby, B., 97

Oldendorf, W. P., xii, 46, 63-86, 97, 146-150
O'Neil, E., 37
Oscanyan, F. S., 50
Owen, B., 26, 30-32
Owen, E., 27, 28, 30

Paley, V. G., 53-54, 59, 149
Palmer, P., 50
Park, R. E., 9
Peak learning experiences, 47-48
Pedagogical content knowledge, 46-47
Pelton, M., 76-77
Personal development and affect, 83
Peters, T., 139
Philosophy, 82
Physical sciences, 82-83
Pitner, N. J., 12, 98, 104
Pittillo, D., 70, 71-75
Plato, 14
Porter, L. W., 104
Powell, J. P., 28-29, 34, 70, 108, 148
Prakash, M. S., 63-66
Principals' Institute, 26
Progressivism, 64, 65-68
Provincialism, 137, 142
Purdue Teacher Opinionnaire, 41

Radomski, T., 82
Ramsey, L., 31, 38, 39, 42
Ravitch, D., 36
Reform. *See* Educational reform; Teacher reform
Responsibility
  delegation of, 95-98
  nature of, 94-95
Retention, of teachers, 121, 125
Reunions, alumni, 84-85, 105-106
Rinnander, J. A., 46, 52, 54, 56, 57, 93
Robinson, H. F., 31, 38
Robinson, J., 35
Rogers, A., 72-73, 75
Rorty, R., 49
Rud, A. G., Jr., xii, 45-62, 68, 146-150
Rusk, D., 37
Russell, B., 14
Ryan, K., 2, 48

Sanford, T., 36
Sapp, H., 80

Sapp, J., 80
Sarason, S., 94, 132, 148
Sawyer, E. A., 120-121
Saxe, R. W., 2
Schiffer, J., 2
Schlechty, P. C., 59, 68, 120-121, 139
Schön, D., 98
School efficiency movement, 7-8
Science, physical, 26, 82-83
Scientific management, 7-8
Scientific method, 16-17
Self-knowledge, construction of, 53-54
Seminars, standard
  collegiality in, 91
  evaluation by teachers, 77-79, 114-117, 125-126
  global alumni seminars and, 85-86
  "Humans on Earth" program, 68-79
  planning process for, 102
  sample topics, 79-83
  special interest programs and, 84
  summer pilot program, 35-37, 41, 79-80, 115
Sensory experience, 15-16, 142
Sergiovanni, T., 60
Shapiro, K. S., 100-101
Shared leadership, 87
Sharp, A. M., 50
Shea, C. M., xi, 1-24, 102
Sher, J., 45
Sherman, M., 9
Shulman, L., 45, 46-47
Simon, M. R., 104-106
Sizer, T., 46
Skills development, 16-17
Skinner, B. F., 7
Smith, B., 75
Smith, L., 80
Social decision-making theory, 9
Socialization, cultural, 9-10
Sociocultural expression, 18
Special interest programs, 84
Spring, J., 4
Stedman, D. J., 30, 39, 112
Stern, D., 121
Stewart, B., 35-36
Stoltz, R., 35, 36
Strauss, R. P., 120-121
Stress, teachers and, 10
Study circles, 51

INDEX

Summative evaluation. *See* Evaluation, summative
Summer pilot program, 35-37, 41, 79-80, 115
Sweden, study circles in, 51
Sykes, G., 51

Tappan, M., 49
Task Force on Education for Economic Growth, 27
Taylor, F. W., 7
Teacher burnout, 10
Teacher education
  behavioral skills reform approach, 3, 7-8
  cultural reform approach, 3, 8-10
  moral reform approach, 3, 4-7
  problems of historical models, 11
  as teacher reform, 3-11
  as teacher renewal, 12-22
Teacher excellence, 134-135
Teacher institutes, 4-5
Teacher reform
  teacher education as, 3-11
  teacher renewal vs., 2-3
Teacher renewal, 120-122
  aesthetics in, 20-22, 54-56, 58-59, 142
  as basis of educational reform, 59-60
  concept of, 1-3, 29-30
  criteria for philosophy of, 12-15
  educational leadership and, 59-60
  educational reform vs., *xi*
  history of, 2-11
  hospitality in, 56-59
  as moral decision making, 18-20
  rationale for, 46-54
  as remediation, 121, 125
  as skills development, 16-17
  as sociocultural expression, 18
  teacher education as, 12-22
  teacher reform vs., 2-3, 4
Teacher Renewal: Professional Issues, Personal Choices (Bolin and Falk), *xi*
Teachers
  career ladders for, 134-135
  characteristics of, 121
  collegiality among, 92
  commentary on NCCAT program, 125-126
  developmental differences of, 147
  excellent, 8, 147
  intellectual connections and, 135-138
  isolation of, 131-133
  as learners, 45, 51-52, 64-68
  networking among participants, 124-125
  retention of, 121, 125
  roles of, 129-131
  selection for NCCAT participation, 47, 100-101, 122, 134-135
  seminar evaluation by, 77-79, 114-117, 125-126
  status of, 134-135, 147-148
  working environment of, 133
Teacher scholar programs, 83-84
Teachers for Our Nation's Schools (Goodlad), 147
Technical skills development, 17
Thinking, reflective and critical, 49-50
Thoreau, H. D., *vii*
Thorndike, E., 7
Tikunoff, W., 132
Toben, C., 83
Transactional leadership, 104
Travers, R. M., 7-8
Trust, 14-15, 124
Turkle, S., 53

University of Chicago, 8
University of North Carolina (UNC), 31, 38-40, 107

Vance, V. S., 120-121
Vaughan, J., 142

Waks, L. J., 63-66
Walden (Thoreau), *vii*
Waples, D., 8
Ward, B., 132
Warren-Little, J., 121
Watson, J., 7, 9
Webb, R., 10
Western Carolina University (WCU), 31, 32, 37, 38-40
Willard, E., 4
Wilshire, B., 52
Women
  feminine approach to learning, 139
  in moral reform movement, 5-7